1995

W9-BUU-815

IN DUE TIME

The struggles and triumphs of Alabama quarterback

JAY
BARKER

by
Wayne
Atcheson

The Birmingham News

ACKNOWLEDGMENTS

IN writing a book on the life of Jay Barker, certain individuals gave much encouragement and help to make the effort possible. They include Ben Drake, Doug Segrest, Tommy Ford, Mike Williams, John Merrill, Gary White, Pete Hanna, Mitch Smith, Kent Gidley and Randy Kelly.

ISBN: 0-9635413-7-4

Printed in the United States of America

Published by *The Birmingham News*
2200 4th Ave. S., Birmingham, AL 35203

Book design and layout by Lori Leath-Smith

I love the competitor.

I love the guy who just goes out into the arena for the players to compete. There's just something about the competitor.

There's something also about a role model. You youngsters are looking at a role model here in Jay (Barker).

You just don't have any idea how many letters I get daily and weekly. Very few letters do I get that don't say something about Jay Barker.

I was talking to somebody just the other day about how Jay has unashamedly said that he was a virgin. You can't find many college seniors that can say that.

He's a guy that as a starter at the University of Alabama has won 34 games and only lost two.

And yet nobody knows much about Jay Barker; for you see, he's a totally unselfish player. He's not in it for the credit. He's in because he loves to play and compete.

I love Jay Barker. He knows that.

I love what he stands for.

—Gene Stallings
Football Coach
University of Alabama

DEDICATION

Over lunch at Paul Bryant Hall when Jay was a first-semester freshman in 1990, I told him that if and when he became the starting quarterback at Alabama, he would be in high demand. Neither one of us dared to dream that he would become the Crimson Tide's winningest quarterback. With his devout faith in Almighty God, his strong stand against alcohol and drugs, and his stance for sexual purity through abstinence, Jay has become a role model for youth across America. He has received well over 1,000 requests in his college career to share his convictions.

Now, five years later, we have collaborated on a book about his football career, his Christian faith and moral beliefs.

To the youth seeking a role model, this book is prayerfully dedicated.

—Wayne Atcheson

I dedicate this book to my grandmother, Stella Barker, for her love, support and prayers, and to the late Raybourn Barker, for the love he showed to his family and to the Lord. He was my uncle, who always believed in me and Alabama.

—Jay Barker

PREFACE

WHEN I was approached with the idea of writing a book about my life, I was at first a bit apprehensive.

The first thing I worried about was that the book would be just about me and football at Alabama.

My biggest prayer in life is that God will get the glory in every area of my life.

The most important thing I want you, the reader, to get from this book is not about me, but rather my relationship with my Lord and Savior Jesus Christ.

I pray that someone might be encouraged by this book and maybe someone will find the secret to a happy life; and that is a personal relationship with Jesus Christ. I just hope that this book will impact someone's life for eternity.

My biggest fear when a book like this is written is that it gives too much glory to the individual, and hopefully that is not the case. I hope that the love of Jesus comes roaring through the pages.

I also hope that through this book, young people will see that it is OK to dream big and work hard toward that dream. I hope it teaches young people not to get discouraged by circumstances or people around them.

I most importantly pray that through this book young people will realize that they can succeed without getting involved in drinking alcohol and doing drugs.

I also hope that young people will decide to take a stand against pre-marital sex.

I believe that true success in life is having a personal relationship with Jesus Christ (Joshua 1:8-9), and by spending time one-on-one with Him in order that He may make you what He wants you to be.

There is a small booklet that has meant so much to my life that I encourage you to obtain from Campus Crusade for Christ International and study. It is entitled *Have You Heard of the Four Spiritual Laws?*

It drives right to the heart of the relationship that I hope for every person to have with Jesus Christ. It also backs up each point with the appropriate scripture.

This little book takes you from John 3:16 and John 10:10, that talk about God's love and His plan for mankind, to John 14:6, Ephesians 2:8-9 and John 3:1-8 that explain the process that each of us goes through to accept Jesus Christ as our savior.

The booklet has made a difference in my life. If you can't locate a copy, check out the verses I've mentioned.

I believe they will make a difference in your life too.

Jay Barker
1995

TABLE OF CONTENTS

Alabama quarterback Jay Barker eludes Georgia rush in spectacular comeback effort

IN DUE TIME

The game had the makings of a classic.
For Georgia.
It was October 1, 1994. Alabama was 4-0 and Georgia 3-1. On the arm of Georgia quarterback Eric Zeier, a leading Heisman Trophy candidate and the SEC's all-time top passer, rested the hopes of offensive fireworks for a national television audience.

He did not disappoint. With 57 seconds remaining in the half, he had thrown three touchdown passes for a 21-7 lead, and murmurs of discontent spread among Alabama faithful.

Under the lights of a rare Bryant-Denny Stadium night game, 70,123 looked on in anxious frustration. Was Alabama about to crash and burn in front of a national television audience?

Except for a 42-point outburst against a weak Chattanooga team the first week of the season, Alabama had shown little offensive firepower.

With the defense struggling to contain an inspired and confident Zeier, there was little reason to expect Alabama to keep up, much less catch up.

Then something flickered late in the first half. Jay Barker led a 73-yard touchdown march.

Then the defense held.

Only seconds remained before the half. Barker hit Curtis Brown with 17 and 13 yard gains. He nailed Tony Johnson for 26 to the 15.

The clock was down to five seconds.

Michael Proctor kicked a 33-yard field goal to draw Alabama within 11. Last minute luck? A flicker of hope, only to be extinguished by a torrent of Zeier passes in the second half? The late half heroics helped, but few found it cause for true optimism.

How many times had Alabama's defense been the guardian of victory? And was this the night that the defensive magic ran out?

The more important question on this unusually warm autumn night seemed to be about the offense. How long had it been since Alabama really opened it up? *Could* they open it up? Could a suspect offensive line provide enough protection for quarterback Jay Barker to operate?

Barker had shown the ability before. He had the strong arm. No one doubted that. But would the coaches give him a green light? Could he make the crucial decision again that would bring Alabama to victory?

In two seasons as quarterback, Alabama under Barker's leadership had won every game save two: one loss, one tie. They had played both years for the Southeastern Conference Championship, winning one, and earned a national championship.

Yet the line on Jay Barker was that he was careful. Just

careful. He was operating in an offensive system that insisted on "careful." He was a good guy. A moral guy. A strong, spiritual Christian. The kind of fellow that every mother wished her daughter would marry. He wouldn't lose a game for you. But how much rein would he be given to fight for the win? He was not given total rein. He had to start every season fighting for his position just like everybody else. That is the way Stallings runs his program. Barker shouldered the questions and criticism, and seemed to always prevail, even if just by narrow margins.

Thirty minutes remained for an answer.

ALABAMA took the ball to open the second half, and Barker stepped up to his center. His finest hour had just begun.

On that Alabama autumn night, this tall, handsome man from the suburbs of Birmingham put the questions to rest, showed a national television audience that the best quarterback in the stadium did not wear a "G" on his helmet, and in a single moment became a moral role model for America.

ON that first possession, Barker found Toderick Malone in the flat for a 35-yard touchdown to make the count 21-16.

Moments later, defensive back Tommy Johnson intercepted a Zeier pass and Barker worked Alabama close enough for a 35-yard Proctor field goal to narrow the Georgia lead at 21-19.

Zeier did not roll over. He pushed the Georgia offense 67 yards, pitching his fourth TD pass of the night. The Bulldogs were on top 28-19 as the third quarter ended.

Fifteen minutes remained.

Barker hit fullback Tarrant Lynch for 22 yards.

Then Malone got free on a post pattern, and Barker's pass covered 49-yards for a touchdown that made the score 28-26.

Media, players and fans crowd to hear Barker tell Mike Adamle that it was his "due time"

The teams sawed back and forth. Georgia could not score. But it mattered little since Alabama was behind.

Exactly 2:43 remained when a Bryne Diehl punt was whistled dead on the Georgia two yard line.

Alabama held. Georgia punted and from his 49-yard-line with 2:10 remaining, Jay Barker took the game and his future into his hands.

On second and 10, Barker was trapped. He broke two tackles and scrambled 15 yards.

He passed to Tony Johnson for 15 yards more. Three running plays to the center of the field left the ball well positioned for Proctor. He drilled the ball through the goal posts from 32 yards away.

Alabama, 29. Georgia, 28.

As the clock ticked down to its last second, Bryant-Denny erupted. Excited players and fans ran onto the field. Amid the happy chaos, an ESPN television crew found Barker for a post-game interview.

Reporter Mike Adamle yelled into the microphone to be heard above the crowd.

"Jay, unofficially you had 395 yards passing and two touchdowns, and enough escapes to make Houdini proud," shouted Adamle, turning the microphone to Barker's face as the senior quarterback shook his head in amazement. "Tell us your feelings and thoughts on this great victory over Georgia."

His dark hair matted, and face still wet with perspiration, Barker shouted to be heard. "First of all, I just want to thank my Lord and Savior Jesus Christ because I've had so many criticisms and the Lord says in the Bible, 'If you just humble yourself therefore under His mighty hand, he will lift you up in due time,' and this has been due time for me.

"I just thank the Lord so much for the team and defense we have, and the guys who surround me. I can't express how much I love them and I just love to win. It's been a great game for me and it was those other guys giving me the protection up there. The offensive line did a great job all night long for me."

With fans swarming Jay and the interviewer from behind, Adamle got in another question. "Jay, you are now 28-1-1 as a starter. You have talked about how proud you are of your record. Your thoughts on that?"

"Like I said, that's not just me. That's my whole team. I love them to death. They compete with me. We just want to win as many games as possible. We got to put this one behind us now and get focused on the next one."

Then he was gone, running for the dressing room with helmet in hand amid another roar from a crowd that refused to leave.

The next morning, the headline on The Birmingham News sports column of Clyde Bolton read, "This game was one of the greatest ever."

Wrote Clyde, "As I sit here with the crowd still yelling, 15 minutes after the fact, I'm tempted to write that this was the best game I've watched in 40 years of covering football. But to do justice to that judgment would require the luxury of time and contemplation that I don't have. I do believe I can say it ranks in the top five. How could it not?"

Coach Gene Stallings in reflection the following day said, "It had the emotions of a championship game. Somewhat like the locker room after Miami (the 1993 Sugar Bowl)." It would have been a good game to end a season on but this was just the fifth contest of the 1994 season.

THE Georgia performance and the Adamle interview that followed were a watershed moment for Jay Barker. His coaches must have known. And certainly his teammates. Of course, his mom and dad. They already knew.

But on this night, all of America knew. Jay Barker measured up to the ghosts that haunt every Alabama quarterback. Starr. Todd. Sloan. Stabler. Namath.

And if American youth needed a spiritual model, they had one. In his brief moment with Adamle, Barker left no doubt: That real men can talk about morality and their Christian faith with pride and enthusiasm.

FOR the record, against Georgia Barker completed 26 of 34 passes for 396 yards, two touchdown passes and no interceptions. To that point, it was his finest game in an Alabama uniform. It was the second all-time best passing performance in Alabama history. ESPN named Barker their Player of the Game.

The dramatic athletic performances of the Georgia game generated tremendous attention during the days that followed. Interestingly, and even surprising, was the fact that so much attention was also given to Barker's comments about his Christian faith. In Sunday School classes across the nation the next day conversations centered around one question: "Did you hear Jay Barker's witness of his faith after the game last night?"

SPORTS columns during the week addressed Barker's statements. A number expressed amazement at his presence of mind right after the contest to even quote a verse of scripture (I Peter 5:6-7).

Paul Finebaum of the *Birmingham Post-Herald* wrote: "Some people might take exception to such comments, saying a football game is not the appropriate place to discuss one's faith. But listening to Barker, one was struck by what a wonderful example and role model he is to the rest of the nation."

That same day, Doug Segrest of *The Birmingham News* wrote a story headlined, "Barker's faith has rewards at Alabama." In Segrest's interview with Barker on Tuesday after the Georgia game, the quarterback said, "I'm not a religious person. Religion, in a sense, is just a tradition. I consider myself someone who walks in Christ's footsteps. I believe in discipleship. Through discipleship, I can influence lives. The trophies and stuff I've won will eventually sit in a trophy case. But when I leave, I want to leave a heritage."

Radio and television sports shows around the country took up the subject, but to the Barkers, the most meaningful outcome was a much more private affair.

A few days after the game Jerome and Barbara Barker, Jay's parents, received a phone call at their home near Trussville, a northeast Birmingham suburb.

"Our telephone rang a lot as you can imagine," Jerome recalls. "Many were from people we didn't even know who were calling to say how much they appreciated Jay and the statement he made about his Christian faith following the game.

"But one person who called was Scott Blake, a neighborhood buddy of Jay's growing up. They played football together from the time they were five years old. In fact, they were co-captains of the 75-pound league team.

"Anyway, Scott said, 'Mr. Barker, I just had to call you and Mrs. Barker tonight to tell you that I got saved Sunday.'

"He said, 'You remember how Jay would witness to all of us boys in the neighborhood when he was just seven and eight years old. He would tell us if we didn't get saved that we were going to hell. Well I watched the game against Georgia. When it was over they interviewed Jay. The first thing out of his mouth was Jesus Christ and I said to myself, 'There's Jay, he's still talking about Jesus.'"

"'The next week the Lord really dealt with me and I was as miserable as I could be by Friday. I had gotten away from the church. You know I have a blind impairment and if anyone ever needed the Lord it was me. Sunday morning, I got up and I knew I was going to church and it didn't matter where. I called my girl friend and told her I was going and she could go to if she wanted to. We went to the Cathedral Of The Cross and when I walked into the church and heard the music, the tears started streaming down my face. They were having a revival. It seemed like everything the preacher said was directed straight toward me. I felt like there was not another person there but me that he was talking to.

"'Mr. Barker, I couldn't wait until they gave the invitation hymn. When they did, I stepped right out, went down the aisle and gave my life to Jesus. I just wanted to call you and Mrs. Barker tonight to tell you...I'm so grateful and so happy about this. It all goes back to Jay and the influence he's had upon my life.'"

"...I just want to thank my Lord and Savior Jesus Christ because I've had so many criticisms, and the Lord says in the Bible 'If you just humble yourself, therefore under His mighty hand, He will lift you up in due time,' and this has been due time for me."

—Jay Barker
Oct. 1, 1994 following 29-28 victory over Georgia

Young Barker, the fisherman, shows off a proud catch in the kitchen of his home near Trussville, Alabama

A CHRISTIAN
HOME

*I*t was 1972. Center Point was Birmingham's fastest growing suburb. In a decade it had grown from a few homes and stores scattered along Alabama 75 to the largest unincorporated city in the state.

Homes were going up so fast that dead-end streets were everywhere. Builders would go as far as they could, build homes along a street as far as their credit allowed, sell the homes, then build some more.

Sometimes a builder would come along and turn the dead end into a cul de sac. Sometimes they would open the dead-end to a through street.

Jerome and Barbara Barker were young parents with their own home on Thirteenth Avenue in Center Point. Daughter Andrea was toddling and Barbara was expecting their second child.

Thirteenth Street was a dead-end. Traffic was slow and light. A great place to raise children. "We thought it would always be that way," said Jerome.

On July 20, the Barker's second child was born. A boy. They named him Jay.

Soon afterwards Thirteenth Avenue was opened up and student traffic from nearby Jefferson State Junior College turned their street into a major thoroughfare.

The Barker's worried about their children playing so near the busy street. Their dog was hit twice and so badly injured that it had to be put to sleep.

The issue pushed the Barker's to find a quieter neighborhood and a larger home. With two children, the little house on Thirteenth was crowded.

New homes were going up at a furious pace in the woods and farms that separated Center Point from Trussville. It was in one of the new subdivisions that the Barkers found the brick home that they had been looking for.

It was a big house. Payments were double what they had been with the house on Thirteenth Avenue. In fact, Jerome's boss at the auto dealership where he was working told Jerome he thought the purchase would be a mistake and urged him to reconsider.

But Jerome was certain. And so they moved to the new brick home. It is where they have raised Andrea and Jay Barker. It is where they came to develop a strong Christian faith that has guided the Barker family through the college football experience that has spanned the past five years; an experience that they could not even have guessed of twenty years ago when they moved in.

JAY Barker was dedicated to the Lord before he was born, says Barbara.

BARBARA Barker had become a Christian in June of 1971. She was 28 years old and had been in church all of her life.

Even with all the church background and dedication to teaching high school girls in her church, Barbara said she had missed knowing the Lord in a personal way. She had joined the church at 11, was baptized and was faithful in attending church.

After she and Jerome married, they attended church regularly together.

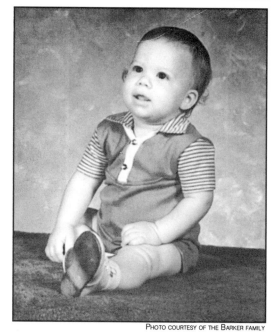

PHOTO COURTESY OF THE BARKER FAMILY

Studio portrait of Toddler Jay

Their daughter, Andrea, was born in 1969 and Jerome and Barbara were careful to raise her in the church. They thought they were doing all the right things to bring their child up in the church, but one thing was missing. They had not accepted Jesus as their personal Savior, Barbara said.

WHEN Barbara was 28 and Andrea was two years old, Barbara's uncle, Sam Cargo, explained to her what it meant to "have a personal relationship with God through his Son Jesus Christ," and how she could establish her own relationship with Him.

He gave her a copy of the *Four Spiritual Laws*, a small book of scripture and direction on how to be saved. Barbara said she gave her life to the Lord and that it was the beginning of the Barker home becoming Christ centered and the basis that Andrea and Jay would be guided down in their home life.

Barbara said she remembers praying for a son who would be a man after God's own heart. She said she spent many hours studying the Bible and praying, and when Jay was born she knew that he had been prayed over and dedicated to the Lord even before he was born.

Barbara said that a year after she was saved, Jerome gave his life to the Lord. Barbara said, "We came to the realization that we were sinners by birth. (Until that time), we always thought that we were okay, because we had not committed sins that we thought were bad enough to send us to hell.

"However, we now had seen scripture that showed us that all have sinned and come short of the glory of God. (Romans 3:23) and that the wages of sin is death (Romans 6:23). How could we have missed this truth when we had been so faithful to go to church? We were known as one of the finest Christian couples in our town, but we had missed the most important person, Jesus Christ. Now we had come to Christ and received him into our hearts by faith, and you know what? He came into our lives, and the Bible says that He will never leave us nor forsake us. What a comfort that is to us as individuals and a family."

"JEROME and I began to study God's word and became very involved and active in Faith Chapel, a non-denominational church. It's congregation met in an old home that was converted into a church facility. It was here that the Lord laid the foundation for our family life and the accountability to the scriptures which would direct us in raising our children to be children who loved the Lord with all their hearts.

"After supper and before TV, we would have a Bible study at our kitchen table. Studying the Bible became such an important part of mine and Jerome's life as a couple and individually. We would read to our children from the Bible before they went to bed and always prayed over them and with them."

"When Andrea learned to read, we would have her read the scripture," says Jerome in retrospect. "When Jay was 5, he was more of a listener at Bible Study time, but could always pray the sweetest prayers even at that tender age. He was sitting there absorbing a lot more than we realized. One night he started asking questions. 'How can someone so far away come to live in your heart?' Jay asked one night during Bible study.

"So at that point, I shifted our Bible study to John 3:16, and God's plan of salvation was read to Jay through many other scriptures. I began to explain the sin nature of man and that each person must come on his own to Jesus and ask him into his heart. It was then that Jay said, 'Well, that's what I want to do, Daddy.

"Realizing that he was only five years old, I told him, 'Son, you need to pray about this and we will pray with you.' Even though Andrea had become a Christian at age five, we wanted to make sure that Jay understood as much as he could at that same age about what it meant to ask Jesus into his life," Jerome said.

TWO or three days went by and Jay would overhear his Mom talking about Jesus to friends over the telephone who were involved in Christian Women's Club, a national organization that Barbara had chaired for the previous four years.

"This ministry instilled many lasting qualities in our family life," Barbara recalled. "Even today, Jay will comment when sharing his testimony about the fact that his Mom was on the phone praying and sharing about the Lord when he was a youngster, and that instilled many strong convictions in Jay about sharing Jesus."

"Preparing meals, helping with homework, having neighborhood kids over to swim and play and doing chores with kind and loving attitudes toward each other was so important in our home," said Barbara.

A few days later, Jay approached his mom about asking Jesus into his heart.

"I had led Andrea to the Lord when she was five, and how precious and special that was to me. I wanted Jerome to have the blessing of leading Jay to the Lord," says Barbara. "I had read the scriptures on salvation with Jay that afternoon and talked to him again about how Jesus went to the cross and shed his blood for our sins and that we could live forever with Jesus in heaven. And just as important was the living for Jesus now in this life. I knew now that the Lord was speaking to Jay and that he really did understand, and wanted to ask Jesus into his life. When Jerome got home from work, Jay said to him, "Daddy, I've talked with Mom and we have prayed about it and I want to ask Jesus into my heart."'

"I said, 'If you are ready, let's go back to your bedroom,'" Jerome recalls. "We went back and Jay knelt down by his bed, prayed and asked Christ into his heart. It was one of the happiest moments I have ever had as a father, knowing that he was going to be there in heaven throughout eternity."

"There were many happy tears at our home that night. Andrea was so excited as were Mom and Dad and now our family was complete in Christ. We had all asked Jesus to be our Lord and Savior.

"Andrea and Jay were both five years old when they came to know the Lord. It was a very young age, but our pastor, Bill Prince, assured us that they had seen Jesus in our life as parents and that they hungered to have what we had even if they were so young. He reminded us that Andrea's salvation was real at five and had been evidenced by her love for the Lord and that we would also see that in Jay's life. He said, 'You will see the fruit in their lives even at this young age.'"

It didn't take long before the bearing of fruit took place after Jay's commitment to Christ. "Jay began to tell his friends in the neighborhood, 'I've got something special to share with you,'" recalls Barbara. "By the time Jay was eight years old, he had witnessed to every boy in our neighborhood.

"As a kid, Jay was always real rough. One day, he went over to a neighbor's house and pinned two boys against the door of their house and said, 'If you don't accept Jesus Christ right now, you are going straight to hell.' The boys' mother called and she was laughing. 'Barbara,' she said, 'Jay has my boys pinned up against the front door and is telling them they are going to hell if they don't ask Jesus into their lives right now.' When sharing his testimony today Jay always includes this incident and says, 'I was a radical for Christ at a young age.'"

"So I got Jay home and told him, 'Son, we don't witness to our friends like that. You have to share Jesus out of a heart of love.' It was funny in one sense, but on the other hand, Jay loved these guys and was sincere in wanting them to ask Jesus into their heart. He wanted his friends to go to heaven with him and not to hell even if he had to use his rough tactics to get them to listen."

"But the neat thing about Jay is that he was vocal about his faith early on. By the time he was eight, he had read the *Four Spiritual Laws* to his friends in the neighborhood and at school. He would ask them, 'Have you accepted Jesus Christ?' Now he was asking in love and knowing that the Lord was going before him in every situation. He knew that the Lord was with him whether in the neighborhood, at school or playing and he took every opportunity to share his faith.

"Jay had such a heart for the Lord from the time he accepted Christ," said Barbara. "Even today, people will talk to Jerome and me about how bold Jay is in expressing his faith. We use these opportunities to share with parents how Jay was saved at five and nurtured in his faith in his home and church.

" We are quick to encourage parents not to depend on the local church to mold their children but to start first in the home and build a solid and firm foundation from the scriptures and to let their local church be confirmation to their children of what they have first been taught in the home. We strongly believe in the local church and its place in our family life, but we first believe that the responsibility of teaching children about Jesus should start in the home. This means that we as parents must be accountable to scripture and love the Lord with all our heart in that our children will not just 'hear the talk but will know that we walk the walk.'

"We know that only by the grace of the Lord can we be the parents that the Lord intends for us to be. We cannot take the credit for our children's love for Christ. They fell in love with the Lord and have chosen to walk closely with him. Our thankfulness for our children and our home life has to go back to that day when Jesus came into my life and a year later into Jerome's life. Jesus has made a difference In our home. We believe that the family that prays together stays together. We have not had a perfect home but we have had a forgiving home which is made perfect in Christ."

"...We believe that the family that prays together stays together. We have not had a perfect home but we have had a forgiving home which is made perfect in Christ."

—Barbara Barker

The chance to play at Legion Field in the Shug-Bear Bowl was a thrill for the young Barker

BEGGING TO PLAY FOOTBALL

*J*erome Barker's father died when Jerome was 9 years old.

That fact was important in guiding Jerome's relationship with his son.

Since Jay pulled on his first uniform at age 5, Jerome has missed only one of his son's games. And he can still tell you that it was a baseball game and that Jay was 10 years old at the time.

At 6-1, stocky and with an air of physical strength, the appearance of Jerome today hints that athletics have long been an important part of his life. In fact, he was a high school all star and played organized basketball until he was 40.

So when Jay fell into those athletic footsteps, the relationship that Jerome could never enjoy with his own father blossomed with his son.

"When Jay was a kid, he was husky, big and just strong. He was always aggressive. We would play games together and he couldn't stand to lose. It would make him so mad when I beat him," Jerome says fondly.

"We started out arm wrestling, and we did that all the time. I would never let him beat me. Barbara would say, 'You ought to let him win some.' I said, 'When he gets older, nobody is going to let him win. He's going to have to win on his own.' So I never did let him win. I told him that when the day comes that you beat me, we won't do it anymore."

"WHEN he was 5, he came to me and said he wanted to play football. I said 'Jay there is no way. You are too young to play football. You need to wait until you are 9 or 10 and grow a little bit more.'

"That didn't stop him. He kept asking. Every day when I came home he would say, 'Dad, I want to play football. All these kids in the neighborhood are playing football. Why can't I play?' I said to him, 'Son, if you ask me again, I'm going to take you to the bedroom and give you a spanking.' Then he starting crying.

"I told Barbara there was no way I was going to let him do this. He kept on asking. Finally, I said, 'I'm going to have to whip this kid every day or either I'm going to have to take him up there (Center Point Metro Park). I know when I take him that he will decide then that he doesn't want to play this. So finally, I said, 'OK Jay, I'm going to let you try it.'

"So I went up there with the intentions that it wouldn't last long. He would at least stop pestering me about it. We went up to the practice, met the coaches and signed him up. I was sitting there talking with some of the dads. I knew a couple of them.

"All of a sudden, I heard one of the coaches say, 'Look at that kid yonder.' They had instructed the kids to run down the field, turn at the goal posts and come back up the field. Well, when I looked up, I knew who they were talking about. It was

Jay. He was 30 to 40 yards on the way back up the field and the other kids had not made the turn yet. Then I overheard one of the coaches say, 'Can you believe how fast that kid can run?' That didn't surprise me because he always ran everywhere he went anyway.

"AFTER practice the coach said to me, 'Now we have got to get him some shoulder pads and a helmet.' The coach told me that he had some pads that he would sell me. He brought the shoulder pads out and I thought they were much too big. Anyway, we put them on him and tightened them up, put his jersey over them and boy they did look big. In fact, he played in those same shoulder pads for the next five years. Then I got

PHOTO COURTESY OF THE BARKER FAMILY

A six-year-old running back, Jay earned the nickname Little Czonka for his hard-nosed style

him a helmet, a good one with the air pockets in it.

"They said they would start hitting the next day and I figured he wouldn't like this and he'd be ready to go home. Barbara took him to practice that day and I pulled up after the practice had started.

"I looked out there and they had him at fullback. They gave him that ball and he'd move through that line, would keep those legs going and he'd hit and hit and just keep on going. He would get up after a tackle, run back to the huddle, eager to run some more, and just loving every minute of it.

"After awhile one of the coaches said, 'Jay, get over there at linebacker.' And another coach said, 'Let's see what he looks like there.' Some kid comes through there and Jay hit him and I thought he had broken every bone in his body. Then one of the coaches said, 'Can you believe how that kid can hit?' Then I said to myself, 'Oh my goodness, I have made a mistake.'

"I took him home that night and I told Barbara it didn't work. It backfired on me. In his first year on the team, his nickname was 'Little Czonka', after Larry Czonka who was the great fullback for the Miami Dolphins at that time.

"THE first game they played was Gardendale. They handed him the ball

At 7, Jay and dad, Jerome, were involved in several sports at Metro Park

on their own 20-yard line and he hit the hole and just kept on going. There was nobody in 10 or 15 yards of him when he stepped in a hole on the 10 yard line and fell down. The next series of downs, they give him the ball on second down and he just goes again all the way down the field for a touchdown. He was so much faster than the other kids.

"There were other teams that were bigger and stronger. Some of the kids were afraid, but Jay would always say, 'Give me the ball, I'll carry it, I'll carry it.' The harder they hit, the better he liked it."

SO from the age of 5, Jay seemed destined for football. At 7, he began to play baseball. The next year, came basketball. From the time he was 8 until 11, his basketball team didn't lose a game. It was coached by his father, Jerome, who had been an all-state basketball player at Tarrant High School, recruited by several colleges and asked to walk on at Alabama by then Coach Hayden Riley.

Jay's aggressiveness showed on the court as well. "We were ahead of this team 25-0," recalls Jerome. "So I told our boys to stay in the square on defense. We had been playing with a full court press. I looked out there and four of the boys were in the square, except Jay. He couldn't stand staying inside and giving them a chance. He was out there attacking the ball. So I had to bench him for two quarters to teach him a lesson. That was just the way he was."

Jay and sister, Andrea, pose by a Florida orange grove on vacation; antics that made Andrea laugh kept young Jay in hot water

A STRONG
WILLED CHILD

*J*ay Barker may have given his soul to God and his heart to athletics, but irresistible yearnings of a strong will and mischievous spirit kept him in hot water at home.

"Jay was a very, very strong willed child," recalls Jerome. "He got a lot of spankings and most of them came from sitting at the kitchen table at night eating supper; a lot of them because Jay was a big cut-up. Jay loved to cut-up and...make his sister, Andrea, laugh at him at the table.

"Being raised like I was, one of ten kids, we couldn't talk when we came to the table," said Jerome. "We could ask for someone to pass the biscuits or something, but with six or seven kids talking at the same time with your parents sitting there, we just didn't talk that much.

"However, with our family, I didn't mind them talking as long as we were carrying on a conversation. But Jay would get to doing stuff that would make Andrea laugh and I would tell him, 'Now Jay, son, that's it. That's enough.' But then he would just keep doing it. So finally I would just have to excuse us from the table and take him to his bedroom and spank him.

"I used a belt and when I would get through spanking him, I always told him that I loved him and we would have prayer before we came out of the room. I would always tell him too that this hurts me more than it does you.

"Jay got spankings for other things like when he wouldn't come home on time or wouldn't do things he was suppose to do. I was just a firm believer in discipline and that was the way I was raised. I believe in 'Yes Sir' and 'No Sir' and 'Yes Ma'am' and 'No Ma'am'. I believe in that.

"But one time we were sitting at the supper table and for several months I had kept giving this kid spankings for the same thing, and that was cutting up at the table. So finally one night, I said to myself that I know Jay doesn't love these spankings because I know it hurts him.

"So we started back to the bedroom. I told him that this was about the tenth time for spanking him for the same thing. I took my belt off and, of course, he knew what was coming. He turned around and I said, 'Turn back around Jay' and I handed him the belt. He looked at me and said, 'What are you doing?' I said, "Evidently as a father, I have failed you. I just can't get over the point of what you are doing wrong, therefore you are going to spank me.'

"He said, 'Daddy, I'm not going to spank you.' And I said, 'Yes you are because if you don't, you are going to get the worst spanking you've ever had in your life.' So I turned around and I said, 'Hit me.' He hit me with a light tap. I said, 'Jay, I mean hit me son or you are going to get a hard spanking from me.' So he hit me a little harder that time, but it still wasn't hard. So finally I turned around and I said, 'Jay, I'm not telling you any more. If you don't hit me like I know you can hit me, you are going to get it and I'm not telling you any more.'

"Well, I wish I hadn't said that because the next time he hit me, I felt like I was coming up off the floor, it hurt so bad. I turned around and I think I had tears in my eyes. He was pretty strong at 11 years old. But when I turned around and he saw the tears in my eyes, he broke down and started crying and that kid cried and cried and cried. He started saying, 'I'm sorry, I'm sorry, I'm sorry.' I kept telling him, 'Jay, that doesn't

The Barkers remained a close family as Andrea and Jay grew into adolescence

feel too good when you have to do something like that, does it? He said, 'No sir it doesn't.'

"He really cried and I think that was when his will was broken that night. I think he finally realized that what I was doing, I was doing it out of love. As the years went by, I would tell my children about people who couldn't learn to respect authority. I said people who can't ever learn to respect authority will end up in prison or thus find themselves living on the streets.

"We would go by the Jimmie Hale Mission on the way to Grandma's house every Sunday and as I would drive by there, I would say, 'Well, you see those people there Jay, they never accepted discipline and never understood authority.

"After that incident, I didn't have to spank Jay much any more. From that point, discipline consisted of curfew or taking away privileges. I think there is a certain age where a parent doesn't need to get a belt and start spanking their child. Other measures are just as effective.

"I'm not saying that Jay wouldn't continue to cut-up, but when I would say, 'Jay that is enough,' well then he would cool it. He knew I meant what I was saying. Still, Jay was so much fun as a kid. He would keep us in stitches.

"He was a pleasure to raise, but when he needed disciplining, he received his share and I know it paid off for Jay and us as parents."

"...Jay was a very strong-willed child. He got a lot of spankings...because Jay was a big cut-up."

—Jerome Barker

Doing things together was an important part of Barker family life; here, they pose for a photo at Pike's Peak

GODLY
PARENTS

*J*erome and Barbara Barker get the question frequently.

quently.

What did they do for their kids to turn out as they did?

Because he has heard the question so often, Jerome has spent time reflecting on the raising of a son and daughter.

Certain things quickly become clear as he talks about the successes and failures that go with raising kids. He had a plan. He drew that plan from his faith. And he stuck with the plan.

JEROME and Barbara nurtured their children in a Christian home and in the church.

"If we had a bad attitude," says Jerome, "Barbara and I would tell Andrea and Jay that we were sorry and ask their forgiveness. There were times when we would ask our kids to do something and maybe they didn't want to do what we wanted them to do. We always had open communication with our kids, though. We talked things out."

"I realized as a young mother that I set the tone for the home," said Barbara. "When Jay first started to school, one morning things were out of balance at home. I knew my attitude hadn't been good. So I told Jay and Andrea when we got into the car, 'You know guys, my attitude wasn't right this morning, and I just want to ask for your forgiveness.'

"Then I began to sing a little song that we sang a lot on the way to school which was, 'This Is The Day, This Is The Day, That The Lord Hath Made, That The Lord Hath Made. I Will Rejoice, And Be Glad In It." Only on this particular morning, Jay didn't sing because he was still a little upset. But I kept singing and about halfway to school, he started singing along, kind of soft at first. Then by the time we got to school, he was screaming at the top of his voice, 'This Is The Day That The Lord Hath Made. I Will Rejoice, And Be Glad In It.'

"That song has been so precious to our family," said Barbara. "Our kids grew up knowing that any moment you can have a bad attitude, but you can give it to the Lord, ask for His forgiveness, and go on and not dwell on it."

THE Barkers took advantage of every opportunity to warn against the dangers of peer pressure.

"The reason I told Andrea and Jay these things was because even though teenagers are Christians, they don't have the wisdom that their parents obtain over the years.

"When Andrea turned 16, I just sat down with her and told her that she was not responsible to me anymore in a lot of areas in her life," Jerome said. "I told her that she was a Christian and that she had Christ living within her. After a good father-daughter session together, I had a prayer with her and committed her to the Lord Jesus. I said, 'You belong to Him and you answer to Him.' And I told Jay the same thing when he turned 16.

"I told them both that you can tell me anything. You can lie to me, but I said you can't lie to the Lord. I told them that the Lord knows what you are doing whether it be sex, drugs, drinking alcohol or whatever. You are taking Christ with you. I said you can tell me that you don't do these things, but I said you can't tell Christ that you don't do them because He is there with you.

"From that day on, I said that they were not responsible to me anymore but to the Lord. They began to drive, of course, and I told them they would be around people that I wouldn't have any control over, because I wouldn't be taking them where they needed to go.

"If you are around where drinking is going on and people are wanting you to drink, I said just remember when you take a drink, Christ is taking it with you. If you decide to have sex, well Christ is going to have sex with you. Whatever you do, you are taking Him with you. He is not going to leave you while you are drinking, having sex or taking drugs and come back when you are through with it.

"I won't take credit for that wisdom and advice, because Dr. Charles Stanley (pastor, First Baptist Church, Atlanta) is where I heard that back when Andrea and Jay were young. Even today, I will have some of Jay's friends say to me that when Jay went to a party at 15, he refrained from those temptations. Some nights when he was at a party and drinking would be going on, he would call me and say, 'Dad, would you come and pick me up.' When he started driving and would get to a party where drinking was going on, he wouldn't stay there."

Barbara remembers a locker room encounter in the eighth grade. "The first time Jay was approached, it was in the locker room and some kids asked, 'Jay, have you had sex?' Startled by the question, Jay asked 'What, what are you talking about?' They began to confess things that they were doing and

Jay started talking about Jesus with them.

"There was one boy who had asked Jay that question and as Jay was telling him that 'I don't chose that because of my relationship with Jesus Christ,' another little boy was just sitting to the side listening. That little boy came to know Christ with Jay the next day.

"Still, he was always accepted," Barbara said. "He never looked down on other kids because they were drinking."

Jerome says he used a quote he heard once to further emphasize to Andrea and Jay the importance of making a stand when it was the tough thing to do. "I told Jay and Andrea they had 'to stand for something or they would fall for anything.'

"I would talk with Jay and say the reason that kids do these things was because of peer pressure. The pressure should be on the kids doing the drinking and all that other stuff. I said that as a Christian you shouldn't have any peer pressure because you're different.

"You have Christ living with you. If anything, they are the ones who should have the pressure because they don't have Christ living within them. If they did, they wouldn't be doing the things they are doing. I always told both of them to be different. Don't be like the crowd; be what Jesus wants you to be."

Perhaps that acceptance by his peers had to do with not being judgmental. Whatever the reason, an incident near the end of the eighth grade told Barbara that her son's moral stand was not costing him friendships.

"His eighth grade class chose favorites like Best All Around, Best Liked, Best Looking, Most Studious and so on," she said. "He got a call and was told that he had been nominated for all ten favorites. They told him he could chose two things. So Jay informed them that he would chose only one and he chose Most Athletic."

"...I always told (Jay and Andrea) to be different. Don't be like the crowd; be what Jesus wants you to be."."

—Jerome Barker

PHOTO COURTESY OF THE BARKER FAMILY

At 12, Barker was wearing the jersey number of his favorite college star, running back Major Ogilvie of Alabama

SIZE 12 SHOE AND FAST AT 12

*W*hen Jay was 12 years old, he wore a size 12 shoe. As a running back in his Metro years, from age 5 through 12, Jay stacked up touchdowns because those big feet were the fastest on the team.

Ken DeLoach, who made his living in construction sales, was Jay's first football coach. DeLoach was 31 the day Jerome Barker brought his son to the Metro park to drain the passion for football out of his son's system. DeLoach was there because he had a son named Lance, about the same age as Jay. Like most youth dad/coaches, when Lance became a player, DeLoach became a coach.

"We put Jay at running back because that was our greatest need," DeLoach remembers. "He could have played quarterback from the beginning, but we needed him to run the ball because he was so fast and so good."

What heady stuff for a boy of five. Those broad shoulder pads. A maroon jersey with huge white block letters. Number

27. A running back's number. White pants so that dirt and grass stains stood out. A white helmet lined with battle scars. White socks to the knee and black shoes with plastic cleats. Life could have been no better than football in Center Point, Alabama.

WHEN Jay was 7 years old, the Alabama Youth Football League held its first Alabama Youth Bowl game. It was quite a celebration as 4,000 peewee football players, cheerleaders and parents from throughout metropolitan Birmingham met at Leeds High School stadium.

Playing in the 65-pound championship game, Jay's team shut out Leeds 25-0. Jay scored all three touchdowns. The Center Point Trojans got to the championship game on the strength of a 38-0 rout of Fultondale. Jay had touchdown runs of 40, 35 and 15 yards to lead the way.

Three weeks later on November 13, 1979, the *Birmingham Post-Herald* sports page reported another Trojan game. "Center Point defeated Huffman, 13-6, in Youth League football yesterday, advancing to play Crestwood in Saturday's Shug-Bear Bowl at 9 a.m. Jay Barker scored on a 56-yard run for Center Point's first touchdown and Matt Limbaugh ran 29 yards for the other. Center Point now is 6-1."

Such play on Metro park football fields would become the pattern for Jay Barker as he moved through the 75-pound, 85-pound and 105-pound weight classifications. A 100-yard rushing game was not uncommon. He was a natural with the football under his arm.

"Jay was little when he played Metro football," says DeLoach. "In fact, he would be about 20 pounds lighter than the other kids in his division. It didn't make any difference. He excelled.

"Jay was an extreme athlete. He was probably his own biggest critic. I can remember times when Jay came out and we would try to put in a new play. Jay maybe couldn't grasp it. Practice would be over but Jay would say, 'Show me this, show me that.' He wasn't satisfied until he knew the play completely.

"I also coached Jay in baseball through most of his Metro years. Even in baseball, we would have a game and maybe he didn't perform the way he wanted to perform. Then I would go by his house and there would be Jay and Jerome working on his game in the yard. Jay just strove for excellence with sports as well as his love for the Lord.

"I've never known Jay to participate in anything and go half-way with it. Still I have always believed that Jay's athletic ability is a gift from the Lord. Jay is the type person, whether it be football, baseball or basketball or if he decided to take up sewing, he could be the best at it because he is going to strive to do his very best.

"In my 21 years of coaching Metro sports, I have never seen any other kid do it before, but he was our team chaplain. At the end of every season, we had a little banquet and would give out trophies. We would give Jay a chaplain's trophy each year. When Jay was young, he was not bashful but kind of quiet. You really couldn't get him to talk that much in front of people. When we had the banquet or said our game prayer, that's one time Jay had no reservation, no bashfulness. Praying just came natural to him. At our banquet, we would have about 30 players, their parents, brothers and sisters and some grandparents. When you have a kid who is 8, 9 and up to 12 years old to come up to the microphone before a hundred people and say a prayer as well as he did, that's impressive to me. But Jay did that so well." The young Barker was much more than just a lasting pleasant memory. The Barkers said that DeLoach had told them that the witness of their family had led him to commit his life to Christ several years ago.

JAY'S dad had always been an Alabama fan and it rubbed off. "Jay had pictures of Coach Paul Bryant in his room and that quote of his which said, 'If you believe in yourself and have dedication and pride and never quit, you will be a winner. The price of victory is high, but so are the rewards.' In 1978 and 1979 when Alabama was winning the national champion-ships, Jay was 6 and 7 and already had his sights on going to Alabama. He changed his number from 27 to 42 because Major Ogilvie, Alabama's star running back, wore that number on his jersey.

"JAY drove himself even in those early years. While other kids were watching television, riding bicycles and going to movies, Jay worked on improving his athletic skills," said Jerome. "He was always running and would mark off 40 yards in front of our house from a neighbor's driveway, and run sprints trying to improve his speed. Somebody told him that if you jumped off and on boxes that your speed would improve. When Jay was 5, I built an 18x36 swimming pool in the back yard. I told Jay that if he jumped on the diving board as if he was jumping on and off of boxes that it would have the same effect. One night, I heard something out back and there was Jay jumping on the diving board until he wore out.

"In fact, many nights until late, Jay would swim laps to improve his stamina. He was always doing pushups and constantly working to better his athletic skills. He played ball year around. Not only were football, basketball and baseball favorites of his, but he ran track and still holds records at the Metro park in Center Point."

Metro park and Center Point Sports Association became an important part of the Barker's family life. In 1979-80, Jerome was president of the Sports Association. "We raffled off a car and improved our concession sales which allowed us to just completely renovate the Metro park which has about

20 acres. More playing fields were constructed. The fields were manicured for better playing conditions. Concession stands were built. Parking lots were asphalted. We just had a beautiful place for about 1,200 boys and girls to play sports. We ended up with six diamonds and one football field. Half of the players would eventually go to Erwin High School and the other half to Hewitt-Trussville."

Years have passed since Barker suited up in the name of a Center Point Metro park team. But officials there still are proud of the Barker name and the Barker family role in the park's development and growth.

As a reminder, in 1994 a new sign was erected at Gus Tucker Field. It reads, "Home of Jay Barker."

AT 13 Jay entered Hewitt-Trussville and became vice-president of his 8th grade Student Government Association. Leadership seemed to come natural.

He joined the school choral group, and performed in long sleeve white shirt with cuff links, black bow tie, black slacks and shoes. Singing for school assemblies and county and district competition was fun and helped balance athletic interests.

Jay played football on the B-team in the 8th grade. The coaches were new. The players were new and a 1-6 record was not something Barker would ever learn to endure well. But that one victory provided a hint of Jay's future as a football player:

In the 1986 *Triumph*, the junior high school annual, several players wrote their favorite memory of the season. Beside his football face shot, Jay wrote: "It was Friday afternoon at about 4:30 and we were down by seven in the fourth quarter. The coach and I had talked about running a rail pass route at half time. The time had come and he sent the play in on third down. He had called a rail route pass.

"As I told the team the play, I looked at John Sims and said, 'You can do it,' The whole team looked as if they had the determination to win the ball game. When I approached the line all I could hear were the people in the stands cheering. I called out the signals and Alan Spooner snapped the ball. It was a perfect snap. I dropped back about three steps and threw it right into the arms of John Sims. He caught the ball and took off for the goal line. When I saw him catch the ball, I took off right behind him. It was a 52-yard touchdown. Everyone was so excited.

"We were down by one; so we went for two. Coach (Mark) McCaleb decided to run the same play again! This time the pass was not very pretty but it hit John in the hands and was good for two. We held them and won the game!"

On the inside cover of that same annual, a fellow student wrote a prophetic note : "Hey, well ever since I met you, I have always thought you were very special! Allow God to direct you and you will go far! He has special plans for you!"

"...If you believe in yourself and have dedication and pride and never quit, you will be a winner. The price of victory is high, but so are the rewards."

—Paul Bryant quote on plaque in Jay Barker's room

Barker's body had caught up with his big hands and feet by the time he was playing for Hewitt-Trussvile High School

JAY AND THE HIGH SCHOOL YEARS

*A*s a ninth grade quarterback at Hewitt Junior High School, Barker stood five-feet, four-inches tall, weighed 135 pounds. In the choral group school annual picture that year, everyone in his row was taller than he was. Most of them were girls.

But Barker could grip a football. He always had big hands and big feet. He kept hoping that the rest of him would eventually catch up.

It was about that time that Barker began to experience pains in his knees. It was a frightening situation. "I had no idea what was going on," Barker remembers. Growing pains had taken their grip. In a little over a year, he was 5-11 and 163 pounds, and as a senior he had grown into a 6-2, 195-pound frame that surprised even Barker and his parents.

"When I first met Jay, Barbara and Jerome brought him by the baseball field when I was coaching at Huffman High School," said Coach Phil English, who later became Barker's high school baseball coach and was the dean of high school diamond coaches in Alabama. "Jay was about 14 at the time. He was short, black headed and was kind of a thin boy. Our top player was Phillip Doyle.

"The next year at Hewitt, I was working behind the concessions stand at our first basketball game. I decided I was going to go in and watch some of it. There was this kind of thin kid on the varsity. He looked kind of familiar and I said to the person next to me, 'Boy, that kid has some talent.' He said, 'Well, you know him.' And I said, 'No I don't know him.' My friend said, 'That's Jay Barker. That's Jerome's son.' Startled I said, 'What! I just saw him last year. He wasn't this tall. He must have grown a whole foot in a year there. But he was the only tenth grader who was playing on our varsity basketball team.

"During the spring, he came out for baseball and made our team. He was the best athlete in that class by far. He played shortstop on our B-Team and by the end of the year, he had moved up to the varsity squad."

As a tenth grader in football, Barker was the B-Team quarterback in an option offense. He also dressed out for the varsity games and played some at free safety and wide receiver. "Jay developed late physically," says Coach Jack Wood, his high school football coach. "He seemed half the size of the other players in junior high and was still relatively small as a tenth grader. But I looked at those big feet and felt that one day he was going to grow into them, which he did. Also, as a tenth grader, he was so attentive in the quarterback meetings which coaches delight in. We pick up on that kind of interest.

"As a junior, Jay could have been our quarterback if we had needed him at that position. We had a senior quarterback and usually we go with seniors. Since Jay was such an outstanding talent, we needed him most at free safety and wide receiver. He was an outstanding free safety and was about as good as we've ever had." Small colleges started talking to Jay his junior year as a defensive back.

As the little kid began to grow, other good things began to happen. "Jay wanted to get more distance in his throwing the football," remembers Coach English. "I said to him, 'Well, you are trying to muscle up. You can't let your muscles tighten up to get more distance. Just get more body rotation by pulling that left arm and all.'

"Boy, he picked that up in a minute. He began to follow through straight down with his throwing arm, he began to get the right trunk rotation and the next thing I know, he's zipping that ball 70 and 75 yards without any effort at all. He was throwing spirals, too."

That summer, other people from outside Trussville began noticing Barker's quarterback potential. The Bowden Academy for quarterbacks and receivers was at Samford University. Coach Bobby Bowden and his sons Terry and

Hewitt coach Jack Wood works with Barker, his senior quarterback

Tommy were running the camp which included a football throw for distance. Staged in Samford's Siebert Stadium, Barker stepped up and threw 68 yards on his first throw. His second pass went 70 and his third was for 73 yards, which still stands as the record in the Bowden camps. Dameian Jeffries, a big tight end from B.B. Comer in Sylacauga, threw the ball 65 yards and would later become an All-Southeastern Conference defensive end for the Crimson Tide with Barker. "I learned valuable lessons in the fundamentals of the quarterback position at the camp," remembers Barker. "I would also go to Samford all during the summer and throw with Jimbo Fisher, Samford's outstanding quarterback, and he taught me a lot."

In Barker's senior season for the Hewitt Huskies, the team ran an option offense, mostly a running attack. However with Jay's strong arm, the team passed with good success. Barker threw for an average of 13 passes a game, which was high compared to past seasons. On the year, he completed 82 of 142 passes for 1,320 yards and 12 touchdowns. College recruiters now started looking at Barker for his offense. They knew he was a top free safety, which he played almost every down that year as well.

Hewitt had a regular season of 6-4 and defeated Huffman 22-7 to earn a spot in the state 6-A (large schools) playoffs. In that game, Barker ran for a third quarter touchdown and junior Dane Prewitt, who went on to kick for the Miami Hurricanes, punched through a field goal. Their team eventually lost to Anniston High School, which was quarterbacked by Steve Christopher, who also later signed with Alabama.

"We played very well together because we were close," Barker wrote in the school annual. "We made some of the goals we had set for the season, but we had some games we should have won. We were better than our record."

*Barker, back row center, was popular among students
at Hewitt-Trussville high*

STILL, Barker had made his mark as a football player. He had suddenly blossomed as a high school quarterback college prospect, even though free safety had appeared to be the position that would earn him a college scholarship.

After the third game of his senior season, Coach Dick Sheridan of North Carolina State offered Barker a scholarship. He fit their style. It was a compliment to Barker so early in the season. He was State's number one quarterback choice. Yet, Barker clung to the dream of playing at Alabama. Film was sent to the Capstone. It saddened Barker that Alabama wasn't showing much interest. Alabama was recruiting two nationally touted out-of-state quarterbacks who had more experience at the position.

WHEN Hewitt played Mountain Brook in the season's sixth game, Pat Sullivan was in the stands watching his son Patrick play. Barker had one of his better games and suddenly caught the eye and attention of the Auburn University coach.

Sullivan began to recruit Barker hard. He wanted Barker at Auburn. The former Heisman Trophy winner saw skills and talent that others didn't see.

As basketball season started, Coach Curly Hallman of Southern Mississippi told Barker, "If it takes me coming to all of your basketball games to get you, I'm going to do it." Hallman came to almost all of Jay's games because Barker reminded him of Brett Favre (now quarterback of the Green Bay Packers), his quarterback at Southern Miss who only played one year at quarterback in high school. Knowing that his interest was Alabama, Hallman said to Barker, "If Alabama offers you a scholarship, you go to Alabama because you will never experience a better school than the University of Alabama."

A discouraged high school athlete now began to seriously ponder attending Auburn, the only SEC school offering him a scholarship. Walking on at Alabama for Barker was not out of the picture.

Then after the 1990 Alabama-Miami Sugar Bowl game, Coach Bill Curry departed for Kentucky and Gene Stallings became head coach at Alabama. A few days later, Coach Mal Moore of the new Alabama staff called Barker and said, "Would you consider giving Alabama another shot?" To which Barker replied, "No doubt about it." Within two weeks, Barker took an official weekend visit to Alabama and was hosted by quarterback Gary Hollingsworth. That Sunday morning, Barker was the first recruit who went in to visit Stallings. When they emerged from his office, Stallings announced to a hallway full of coaches and secretaries, "I've got my first quarterback at Alabama." The group broke into applause. On February 14, the official signing date, Coach Mike Solari came and Barker signed before his family and friends in the high school library.

A dream that was about to slip away had now become happy reality.

Jay Barker was Alabama bound.

A fellow member of Barker's high school debate team wrote in the back of his senior annual. "I'm really glad I got to know you better this year. You've really taken a Christian stand at this school, which desperately needs more people like you. I've been a Christian for years and I find it difficult to take a stand the way you have, but I'm trying. You have been an inspiration to me because of who you are. Stay the same, keep strong in the Lord and please don't let go of what you've got."

Lifelong Alabama fans: Jay Barker and father, Jerome

THE WILL TO PREPARE

*B*arbara Barker was ironing and crying.
A friend, Paulette Roden, was there helping her.

Barker had gone to girlfriend, Amy's, to say good-bye and get over his own anxiousness.

On that day, no one was sure "what I was going into." They remembered the old college freshman hazing stories, and Barker himself was nervous about what kind of roommate he would find waiting at Bryant Hall.

It was college leaving day. It was the first day of Jay Barker's five years as a student athlete for the University of Alabama.

Playing football for Alabama had been a part of Barker family conversations for the better part of a decade.

"We went fishing one day and sitting in the boat, I asked Jay what he wanted to do in his life. He said he wanted to play college football at Alabama for Bear Bryant. I asked him what he thought it would take to be successful. He said most people say you've got to have the will to win, but he didn't think that was it. He said he thought you had to have the will to prepare to win. When he said that, I thought to myself, this kid is going to make it."

For this kid from Trussville, the pushups, sit-ups, sprints, jumping rope and playing ball as long as there was daylight paid off.

NOW that the day was here, Barbara was crying. Amy started crying. With all the emotion, "I was upset too," said Barker.

It was supposed to be an exciting day. Something needed to happen, and it did. In fact, for the Barker family they simply did what came natural to them. "We prayed together. We prayed over me going down there," said Barker. "The Lord gave us all the peace we needed that day to leave for college."

BARKER loaded his Pontiac Grand Prix, said good-bye and drove to Tuscaloosa alone.

It was moving day for everyone at Paul Bryant Hall—America's most famous college football address—and a surreal moment for a kid from the Birmingham suburbs who had dreamed all his life about playing football for Alabama.

"There were faces you had grown up watching play," he said. "It was neat just seeing all those guys."

Barker checked in, drew the assignment of a third-floor room with a guy from Cullman named DeLan Trimble.

Trimble already was there and had chosen his bed when Barker found the room. He remembers Trimble sitting there on the side of the bed holding a basketball and, more importantly, he saw the Bible that sat on Trimble's dresser.

"I came down expecting hellions," said Barker, "but when I got there there were (several) who were committed

Famous faces at Bryant Hall: Barker with Tide running back Chris Anderson

Christians.

"I was thankful to have a Christian roommate. We read our Bibles at night," he said, "and we became good Christian friends."

THE friendship was an important help to Barker's transition to dormitory life. "At first it wasn't comfortable," he said. "Mainly, it wasn't home. Home is home."

At Bryant Hall, two men share each room. At the foot of each bed is a desk. There is a single sink with dressers to either side. Gray carpet. Gray paint over concrete block walls.

The halls were crimson (but since have been painted white).

DOWN the hall were quarterbacks Steve Christopher and Jason Jack, who had led their teams to state champion-ships and were selected for the Alabama-Mississippi All-Star Classic that summer.

"I knew there would be lots of competition when Alabama signed three quarterbacks," Barker says. "But I knew I had potential. That summer, I spent a lot of time at Samford University working out. My mother was secretary to Coach Terry Bowden and he told me I had potential, as well as Jimbo Fisher, their quarterback. Coach Bobby Bowden had encouraged me also. So it became a matter of working hard. My goal was to be a starter from day one."

ASSOCIATED PRESS PHOTO

In early practices, Barker said he was so nervous he could hardly throw a spiral

That fall, Barker began learning from senior Gary Hollingsworth, junior Danny Woodson, and quarterback coach Mal Moore.

He learned from Gene Stallings too. About handling pressure.

Stallings didn't have much in the way of experienced quarterbacks that first fall. He had to find out who could cut it and who couldn't. And fast.

"Coach Stallings wanted us ready," Barker remembered. "He was putting a lot of pressure on."

"I was so nervous I could hardly throw a spiral those first few days," he said.

So he fought through the nerves the one way that had always worked for him before; the way his father said would work.

"My biggest thing was that I wanted to outwork the other person," Barker said. "If we had so many sprints to do, then I wanted to run more than my competition.

"If I ever saw my competition out there working, I always made sure I was out there doing more."

After every practice Barker and receiver Rick Brown would stay 30 or 40 minutes longer than everyone else, throwing and catching. The throws became spirals.

On days when there was no practice, he still was out there throwing, running, working. "I tried to make sure I was the first on the field," he said, "and the last to leave. I still do."

AND all of this was before even Barker thought he could have a chance to play.

"With Gary and Danny there, I really wanted to be redshirted that first year," Barker recalls. "I wasn't ready mentally or physically. However, the only games I didn't dress out for were against Florida, Georgia and Tennessee. When the Auburn game came around, Danny had been suspended. Gary went down in the second quarter. Scott Etter went in and it liked to have scared me to death because I knew I was next. Of course, I hadn't played all year and didn't want to go in really for that year to count against me. Anyway, looking back, I was glad to be redshirted."

EACH January, February and March in the indoor football facility is where Alabama builds championship football teams.

Players anticipate winter drills. With dread.

At 6 a.m. every day each coach awaits players at his own drill station, with his own special form of "torture."

• Three players on the floor. The coach commands the middle player to roll either left or right. The player about to be rolled over must leap the rolling player and, thus, become the middle roller. So it goes, rolling, jumping, rolling, jumping.

• Shuttle runs. Five yards. Ten yards. Five yards. Run. Plant. Run. Again. Again.

• The square. Back pedal. Shuffle right. Forward. Shuffle left. Fifteen yards square.

• Sprints, forward and back.

• Seat rolls.

• Box jumps.

• And the Dreaded Dubose Drill. Named for Coach Mike Dubose. On your feet, moving, moving. Hit it! You drop to all fours. Move it! Forward. Back. Side to side. Back on your feet. Back on all fours. Constant movement.

EACH drill lasts six minutes or so. A whistle blows and players move to the next drill. In an hour it is done.

It gave Barker and the others an hour to shower, dress, breakfast and get to 8 a.m. classes.

"I'VE always had the work ethic, that if you want to be successful you have got to work at it. I've always thought that if you work hard, you expect to be successful," says Barker. "If you are not successful, one can say, well I really didn't work for it anyway. But if you work hard and something happens that you don't make it or become defeated, then you can say to yourself, well I worked as hard as I could, and it won't be as big of a letdown. A lot of people are scared to work for something. What is a shame is to see someone with a lot of ability who refuses to work, therefore they never succeed. That carries over into other areas of their life too, and that's a tragedy to me.

"My dad always told me that I could do anything I wanted to do if I was willing to work and make sacrifices. He told me that the secret was outworking everybody else and I never forgot that. Also, I never wanted to be pampered just because I was a quarterback. The quarterback has to be the leader in every aspect and that definitely includes the conditioning and

Barker congratulates Woodson after a 1991-season touchdown; later that year he would have Woodson's job

weight training programs. It is so important to the whole team for the quarterback to lead the way. But I've always been a fierce competitor and the competition never bothered me."

As spring training began, Danny Woodson was a senior and listed first team. Barker wanted the job, and told Woodson so. "I told Danny, 'I'm really going to fight you for it. If you win, then I want you to have it. But I'm not going to just give it to you.'"

"First was right there," he said. "So why should I settle for second.

"(The conversation) was pretty much straightforward," as Barker remembers it. "It wasn't cocky, but it was a straightforward conversation."

The coming early, staying late, throwing more, running longer, running harder and doing more than anyone asked was the kind of ethic that impressed Stallings.

"Leadership is an important thing to Coach Stallings," said Barker. "Coach is not so much on how you look. He tells us not to confuse activity with accomplishment...that it's not how good you look, but how you're moving the football down the field."

So Stallings watched closely as the physically gifted Woodson and the young Barker battled it out. Which one could keep an offense on the field?

Which could be a field general.

Which could lead men in battle.

Stallings preached to them the things that he knew made winning quarterbacks: That they alone must set the tone for the offense, must have that intuitive judgment to make the right call, the smart call, and to be careful and keep mistakes to a minimum.

BARKER took Stallings' words and wove them into his personality. "One of my biggest things is that I'm not fake with (his fellow players)," says Barker. "I treat everybody in the huddle individually different, but I treat my huddle the same.

"I know I love them," he said, "And I do everything I can for them.

"I never screamed at the guys," he said. "I just tell them that let's do everything we can together."

And the players responded.

"I think the guys respected me, partly because I'm not the prima donna. I think (a leader) always does better with people when he has been one of them.

"I wasn't touted out of high school," he said. "I had been one of them because I had worked so hard and because I was hard nosed."

That certain toughness was an important factor in solidifying his position as team leader.

An important moment that still stands out in Barker's mind happened during summer drills when he and Woodson were locked in combat for the starting position.

"At that time quarterbacks were live game," Barker remembers. "We had this goal line thing we were working on. I took the ball and tried to cut behind (lineman) George Wilson to score."

The linebackers were waiting on Barker. His mouth was a mess. By the time he was back to the huddle he could taste the gush of blood. He spit enough out that he could call the next play through smashed lips.

The team knew then. This guy was going to take the hits with the rest of them.

George Wilson was considered among Alabama's toughest linemen. In an off-season hunting accident he had blown off much of one foot and doctors said he probably would not play again.

He played again. First string.

After the goal-line drill, Wilson found Barker on the

sideline, still bleeding. "Hey man," Barker remembers him saying, "I gained a lot of respect for you out there today. That fired me up."

By the time drills were complete, Woodson was listed first team; Barker, second team. From that moment, Barker never dropped lower on the depth chart.

ALSO in the fall of his freshman year, Barker found something at Alabama as important as the chance to play football for the Crimson Tide.

The Fellowship of Christian Athletes met every Wednesday night at 9 o'clock in the Bryant Hall study room. Jay became an immediate fixture, never missing a meeting. He would read the scripture, explain its meaning, and would be called on to pray.

Other members were impressed by his spiritual maturity. Barker also entered the Athletes in Action ministry and Bible studies that were conducted in the dorm.

These groups provided Barker a base from which to share his faith with teammates, and to offer them spiritual encouragement and guidance. Barker also found others who shared a common Christian faith. Among them were Matt Wethington, Mickey Conn, Roman Colburn, Alan Ward, Martin Houston and Willis Bevelle. They developed a special bond based on spiritual faith, and, from that faith, a special caring about the well-being of their fellow players. These were guys Barker could lean on for support and encouragement.

IN Barker's freshman year, a seemingly insignificant moment as fall training began has come to have special meaning to Jay. "I knew that they would be giving us our jersey numbers that would likely be our number for our career at Alabama," Barker recalled. "I had been praying about my number. I had worn number 11 in high school and when they threw me my jersey with number 7 on it, I was a little disappointed.

"That night at FCA, our speaker gave an overall review of the book of Revelation. When he began telling the meaning of the numbers and that seven meant 'complete' or 'wholeness' and had such spiritual significance in Revelation and throughout the Bible, I knew my prayers had been answered. That's why I'm proud to wear number 7 on my jersey, as a witness unto the Lord in itself."

THE following summer, Barker and other Alabama athletes attended an Athletes in Action discipleship conference at Myrtle Beach, South Carolina. "It was there that I learned for the first time what a powerful influence athletes have. I also learned there what it meant to worship God on the playing field, to have him in your thoughts, to pray, and to be constantly aware of God's presence. The conference also taught me how to stay focused on the field of play and draw strength from the Lord...when I needed something. Those lessons learned there have carried over throughout my entire college career.

"I have always marked crosses on my wrist bands to remind me of Christ as I play, and when I look down at the goal posts, they are a reminder of the Cross where Jesus died for my sins. I have gained strength and confidence, plus poise to stay under control while playing the game from all of this. I'm so thankful I learned those truths and lessons early in my career."

A week before Alabama's first game of 1991 against Temple, Barker edged ahead of Woodson on the depth chart to number one.

Then in the last scrimmage prior to the game, Barker injured his left shoulder. "It was so disappointing," he remembers. "At the same time, it was so satisfying to have reached that level and to know I had a shot at starting. Still, Danny was a senior and a great athlete. We pushed each other to get better and I thought he deserved to play anyway."

In the second game, Barker got a fiery baptism in Gainesville, Florida.

Mid-way of the first half, Woodson came to the sideline holding his elbow.

The young Barker's time had come. Whatever preparation had come before would have to be enough.

Florida led at the half, but only 6-0.

In the second half, the Gators knew they had a new, young and untested quarterback. It was time to blitz. Florida did not disappoint.

In a rain-spattered second half, Alabama fumbled six times and the defense forced Barker into throwing two interceptions as Florida coasted to a 35-0 win. Barker completed 4 of 11 passes for 62 yards, ran for 29 yards on eight carries and caught a pass from Siran Stacy for five more.

Afterwards, Barker reflected on the less than auspicious first outing. "We just have to forget about this and not let it get us down. We learned a lot and it will help us with big games in the future. I'd like to have it back, but we can't."

TODAY, looking back on his first game with the benefit of a time distance, Barker says, "That wasn't the best way to start off and play your first college game at quarterback. My left shoulder was heavily taped up; I couldn't throw good and couldn't move around. But that game put a fire in me to want to win, to be successful, and I knew I could, even though it was a tough loss for us."

Five games later against Tennessee in Birmingham, Barker gave Alabama fans a hint of the future. He entered the game mid-way in the third quarter for Woodson, who went out with a pulled hamstring. Down 6-3 going into the fourth quarter against the eighth ranked Vols, Barker engineered three touchdown scores to put Bama ahead 24-6. The 14th ranked Tide, which saw freshman sensation David Palmer exit the game with a sprained ankle early in the first quarter, held on to knock off Tennessee 24-19.

"I had the jitters when I first went out there," Barker told the media afterwards. "After my first series, I came back on the sidelines and I told the line, 'Look, I've got confidence in y'all. You just have confidence in me, and we'll go out there and ram it down their throats.' I think we knew we could."

Afterwards, Stallings put Barker's performance into perspective. "Jay Barker coming off the bench and taking us on a 70-yard drive was a key series. He hadn't really been getting a whole lot of work."

That game gave Alabama a 6-1 record and sent a message to the Crimson Tide's next four opponents. Two weeks later, Woodson was suspended and Barker got his first start in LSU's Tiger Stadium.

It was a solid, if not spectacular victory. David Palmer raced 90 yards on a punt return for an early 7-0 lead. Alabama tacked on another 13 points before the half, then held on for a 20-17 victory. Who would know that from this point, Alabama would lose but two games and tie but one so long as Jay Barker was the starting quarterback.

Senior co-captain Kevin Turner, who rushed for 144 yards against LSU that November night, talked about Barker's first start. "He played a great game," said Turner. "He had one interception, but other than that, he did a great job. It's always distracting when somebody gets suspended, but Jay stepped right up without missing a beat.

"It's the way he works," Turner continued. "It's the way he carries himself. He's a real leader, a natural leader. He has all the intangible qualities."

And so the season played out with Barker at the helm. He

did what had to be done to win.

The week after LSU, he threw a bomb across the middle to Kevin Lee for a 75-yard touchdown, pulling out a 10-7 win at Memphis State. Then he steadily guided Alabama to a 13-6 decision in the all-important Auburn game in Birmingham. The Blockbuster Bowl in Miami gave Barker his fourth win in four starts as the Tide prevailed 30-25 to finish 11-1 and fifth ranked in the final polls.

It was a high-note ending for a young quarterback. He had not put up big numbers. But he had won his games. And the three second-half touchdowns Barker threw in the close victory against Colorado in the Blockbuster Bowl gave cause for hope that 1992 could be something special.

"…I asked him what he thought it would take to be successful. He said most people say you've got to have the will to win. But he didn't think that was it. He said he thought you had to have the will to prepare to win. When he said that, I thought to myself, this kid is going to make it."

—Jerome Barker

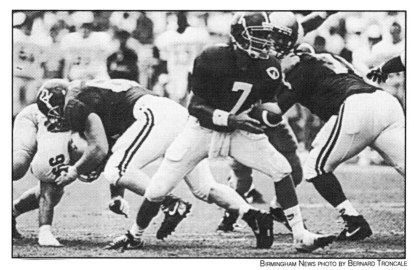

Barker hands off in opening game against Vanderbilt, first contest in the road to the National Championship

NATIONAL CHAMPIONS

The Starlite service was rained out at Berry High School's Finley Stadium, so the Shades Mountain Baptist Church program was moved to its sanctuary on Columbiana Road in the suburban Birmingham city of Hoover. It was July 23, 1992. More than 3,000 gathered to hear the special guest of the evening, Jay Barker, the University of Alabama's 20-year-old redshirt sophomore quarterback.

The annual event, which featured Dave Dravecky, Oliver North, Truitt Cathy and musical groups nightly in a series of services, drew people from across the Birmingham area. It was unusual to hear from such a person so young. However, when you are the quarterback at Alabama, your name is repeated as often, if not more often, as the governor in households, coffee shops and beauty shops of this deep south state.

Barker's turn came, and he strode to the pulpit. Shades

Mountain Baptist's Starlite program is known for the huge crowds that attend. But Legion Field today could not hold the number of people who can recite the message that Barker delivered to the 3,000 that night.

"I've never taken a drink of alcohol," he said. "I've never taken any drugs and I'm a virgin."

And he told them why.

It was a powerful statement and one that Jay has made hundreds of times since. At the end of his message, more than a hundred young people stepped forward to dedicate their lives to Christ in the area of sexual purity. "That was the first time I made that statement before an audience," says Barker. "It wasn't anything new for me to say that because I had established those morals since I was first tested for my moral stand in the eighth grade. I always tell my audiences that I make that statement not in a boastful way, but I believe it can be an encouragement to the young people and that's why I say it."

So Jay Barker had taken his stand. Not before just the 3,000, but before millions across America as newspapers, radio and television stations picked up his comments.

A role model was developing, but on this eve of the 1992 football season, Barker had no way of knowing where it was all going to lead.

The upcoming season was to be special for Alabama. It would be the university's 100th year of football. Books and videos were being published. Celebrations were scheduled. Even more, there was indication that this was going to be a very good team.

How good, only time would tell.

In the spring, Alabama fans voted on their All-Century team. With so many All-Americans, it was a difficult chore. A "Century of Champions Golden Gala" celebration was staged at the Birmingham Civic Center Ballroom July 18. Keith

Jackson, the voice of college football, was Master of Ceremonies as the offensive and defensive squads were presented.

Among the stars was Alabama's young quarterback accompanied by his father, Jerome, and girlfriend, Amy DiGiovanna. Before festivities began, a photographer grabbed Barker and posed him for a publicity shot. Cameras flashed, and Barker smiled broadly, even more broadly than the two All-Century quarterbacks, Joe Namath and Ken Stabler, who flanked him in the picture. Was this the place for a lightly tested sophomore quarterback, posed between two of the greatest quarterbacks to ever play the game?

Or was it an omen.

At that moment, no one could know.

But when that photo was turned into a centennial celebration fan poster the issue was decided, not on the field, but by a photographer snapping a great shot.

Three years would pass before the world would know for sure whether the photographer was right.

BARKER won the right to start the 1992 season under center with a strong spring practice. It was obvious to coaches and teammates that the Blockbuster Bowl three-touchdown-pass performance has boosted his confidence. Brian Burgdorf and Chad Key would be his backups.

Even before the season began, however, many Alabama followers wondered aloud on the talk shows whether Barker could hold the starting job. But *Birmingham News* Alabama beat writer Charles Hollis saw something special that many others did not see:

"There is something about Alabama quarterback Jay Barker that makes you feel good the moment you meet him. It's hard to say why Barker is like that. It might be how he goes out of his way to let you know he isn't anyone special. A big part of it is his faith in God. Church is important to Barker. And

Passing the Tradition

Alabama senior quarterback Jay Barker, pictured between legendary quarterbacks Joe Namath (left) and Kenny Stabler, needs just eight victories to become the Tide's all-time winningest starting quarterback.

UNIVERSITY OF ALABAMA POSTER

This poster pose between former Alabama quarterback greats Joe Namath and Kenny Stabler was an omen of things to come

church is commitment, just like football."

Quoting Barker, "I look at my situation, and I really mean

this...I feel the Lord has blessed me with a platform to carry His word and the opportunity to perform on the field. I'm aware there are so many guys around who talk about the Lord and try to push their faith on you, but I'm not going to do that. I don't want to turn off people with some holier than thou attitude. You can preach by example."

THE pre-season rankings had Alabama number eight in the country. In their first outing, the Tide beat Vanderbilt in Tuscaloosa 25-8. Nothing spectacular. Nothing to be ashamed of. One unusual point for a running team was that Barker threw the ball 27 times, seven more passes than the Crimson Tide threw in any contest the previous season. He completed 14 passes for 185 yards. "It probably was a shock to our fans to see us throw the ball as much as we did," Barker said afterwards. "They're not used to seeing us pass more than we run."

The next week, Alabama got by a stubborn Southern Mississippi team 17-10 in Birmingham and a week later in Little Rock, Barker completed 14 of 17 passes for 192 yards and three touchdowns for a 38-11 triumph over the Razorbacks. Alabama moved to 7th in the polls.

The defense was drawing more credit than the offense. And, in fact, many say it deserved the lion's share of credit the next week against a Louisiana Tech team that was hard to put away. Tech was held to minus 8 yards rushing and 125 yards passing. The Alabama offense managed only 167 yards. David Palmer, reinstated after a three-game suspension, returned a punt 63-yards for a touchdown in the fourth quarter to seal a 13-0 victory.

Rain didn't hinder Alabama in its homecoming game against South Carolina the following week. Alabama led 38-0 at half-time. Barker left the game after the first series of the second quarter and never came back. Burgdorf and Key finished up as the Tide romped 48-7 and moved to 6th in the polls.

Tulane in New Orleans was a 37-0 tune-up for the Tennessee Vols in Knoxville.

On the third Saturday in October, fourth-ranked Alabama faced a Tennessee home crowd of 97,388 and a 5-1 Volunteer team with a burning memory of losing six straight times to the Tide. Alabama relied again on brilliant defensive play and its running game to win 17-10. Barker did what was required at quarterback, giving the ball to Derrick Lassic for 142 yards. Barker threw only 11 passes, completing 5 for 54 yards.

Alabama now had won 17 games in a row, the last 11 with Barker under center. Still, fans grumbled that he and the offensive coaches simply kept the offense under control so the defense could win the games.

The grumbling was about to quiet, if not go away.

The next week against Mississippi in Tuscaloosa, Barker put the ball in the air 39 times, completing 25 for 285 yards. Alabama won 31-10 on the strength of his arm. He was selected SEC Offensive Player of the Week.

Due to a realignment of SEC scheduling with the new East and West Divisions, Alabama returned to LSU—site of Barker's first start—for the second year in a row.

He was sacked six times. The team survived a blocked punt, a safety and six penalties for 54 yards and still cruised to a 31-10 victory.

Alabama was 9-0 and had been ranked third in the nation when something happened on the other side of the country that opened a door for the Crimson Tide. Arizona defeated No. 1 Washington 16-3 and the new poll put Miami at the top and Alabama No. 2.

The two teams were now on a collision course for the national championship.

Yet Alabama had three of its toughest tests of the season

ahead before a possible Sugar Bowl appearance. At Starkville, Mississippi State led 21-20 going into the fourth quarter before Barker stepped forward and hit crucial passes, one for 24 yards to receiver Prince Wimbley, to set up the go-ahead field goal. Alabama survived the scare and came away with a 30-21 victory. Barker hit 13 of 27 passes for 198 yards.

The Iron Bowl with Auburn was next.

With Bill Oliver, Mike Dubose and Jeff Rouzie's defense at the top of every national statistical department, it dominated the Auburn game on Thanksgiving Day and handed the Tigers a 17-0 shutout. It was Coach Pat Dye's last game and the first shutout of his career as a head coach. "This was a great day for Coach Stallings, the Alabama players and fans," Dye said. "If I had a vote for No. 1, Alabama would get my vote." The game was scoreless at half-time, but Antonio Langham had a 61-yard interception return early in the third quarter to get Alabama on the scoreboard and the momentum.

Barker took care of the offense, which netted 199 yards rushing. He passed for only 63 yards.

AT 11-0, the first Southeastern Conference championship game matched the Crimson Tide against Coach Steve Spurrier and the high-powered Florida Gators in Legion Field. A win put Alabama in the Sugar Bowl against Miami in the game that would decide the national championship. It did not matter where the loser went.

Quarterback Shane Matthews marched the Gators 77 yards on the opening drive for a 7-0 lead. Alabama came back to tie the score, and then with 4:49 left in the half, Barker passed 30-yards to Curtis Brown in the end zone to put the Tide up 14-7.

The lead would not last. By the fourth quarter Florida had tied the score at 21, had swung momentum to its side, had the ball and 3:39 left in the game.

Again, the Alabama defense turned out the lights when Antonio Langham picked off a Florida pass in the flat and raced 27-yards into the end zone. Alabama won 28-21 and the Tide had a date for the national championship dance in New Orleans. In doing so, the Tide became the first team in the SEC to post a 12-0 regular season record and win nine conference games.

A looming Miami was another matter. Big, bad, surly, arrogant Miami. "Players who would whip their mothers for the national championship," was the standing joke.

The team that all America knew would annihilate Alabama.

The Hurricanes were 11-0, had won 29 straight games and were going after their second consecutive national championship. Miami Quarterback Gino Torretta had a 26-1 record and had just won the Heisman Trophy. The odds makers said Miami would win by more than eight points.

SOMEONE forgot to tell Alabama.

Every day as the Alabama players prepared in New Orleans, their confidence got stronger. "The team was ready to play when we got to New Orleans," Stallings said. "I didn't have to give a pep talk. I just had to make sure they didn't play the game on Wednesday or Thursday." Not one of Alabama's 145 players missed a curfew or stepped out of line, despite several confrontations with Miami players in the French Quarter.

The media covered every Miami angle: its great team speed, the senior linebackers, the superior passing game, its Heisman quarterback. Barker went virtually unmentioned.

Before leaving the hotel for the game, Jay and his buddies got together for devotion and prayer, as they usually did before every game. It provided them peace and strength to do their best.

Freshman tight end Tony Johnson found himself nervous as he warmed up before the game, when suddenly into his mind popped the words of II Timothy 1:7. "For God hath not given us the spirit of fear; but of power, and of love, and of a sound mind."

As the team was walking into the dressing room before the kickoff, Johnson put his hand on Barker's shoulder and said, "Jay, we are going to win this game. The Lord is on our side."

Regardless of whether it mattered to the Lord, Tony Johnson, who played most of the game, believed it. And from the opening kickoff, Alabama took the challenge to Miami and the rest is history.

The Alabama defense throttled Miami's offense. Barker directed his usual careful, run-based offense. Running backs Derrick Lassic and Sherman Williams picked up touchdowns. Michael Proctor kicked field goals. In total, Alabama held the ball 36 minutes to Miami's 24, rushing the ball 60 times for 267 yards.

Barker, who passed for 1,614 yards during the season, attempted only 13 passes, and completed four for 18 yards.

"I don't worry about the statistics," he said after the game. "My job is to lead. If we win, I'm happy."

The glory went elsewhere. To Lassic, who earned Most Valuable Player honors. To George Teague, who intercepted a pass for a touchdown and who stripped Miami's star receiver in what may have been the most spectacular play in Alabama football history. And to the rest of the Alabama defense that kept Miami in confused shock. The final score, 34-13.

The next day every poll ranked Alabama No. 1. The winning streak stood at 23 straight, 17 behind starter Jay Barker.

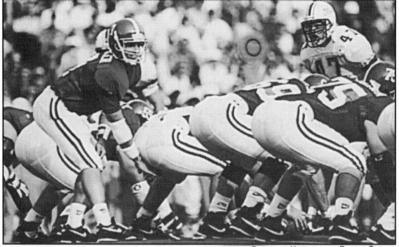

Barker calls signals in opening game against Tulane; the Tide was ranked 2nd nationally but was sluggish against the Green Wave

1993 A SEASON OF PEAKS AND VALLEYS

Squad Sunday at Calvary Baptist Church has been on the Alabama football schedule since 1964. Calvary Baptist sits one block from Bryant-Denny Stadium on Paul Bryant Drive. And each year, one week prior to the first game, players and coaches are seated in the center aisle as regular worshipers arrive early for a good seat.

Jerry Clower, the Southern humorist and outspoken college football fan, was guest speaker. The sanctuary of 1,200 fills fast for the morning service. Students are back for classes and everybody knows that the most important event in town, Alabama football, is just days away.

SQUAD Sunday tops Easter Sunday at Calvary and on this late summer Sunday of 1993, pastor Bruce Chesser renewed a ceremony that is a fixture of the service.

The ceremony has its roots imbedded in the life of

Charley Compton, a rugged Alabama tackle in the mid-1940s who died in 1972 while serving as a missionary in Brazil.

To preserve his memory, the Charley Compton Award was established, and always is presented on Squad Sunday to the Alabama player who has provided the most outstanding Christian leadership on the squad.

The honor is all the more meaningful because the team makes the selection.

The congregation burst into applause when Jay Barker's name was called out by pastor Chesser. Actually, it was no surprise for Jay to be selected. But for Barker and his family, there could have been no greater honor.

ALABAMA went into the football season ranked No. 2 behind Florida State, and got off to a sluggish 31-17 win over Tulane at Legion Field. Barker, however, had a good day leading his team to touchdowns on four of his first five series. He hit 9 of 10 passes for 158 yards including a 59-yarder to Kevin Lee.

The next week in Nashville against Vanderbilt, Barker had an even better game statistically, completing 16 of 20 passes for 279 yards, one TD and no interceptions. David Palmer had eight catches for a school record 217 yards. Yet Alabama came away with only a 17-6 victory.

The following Wednesday night at the weekly Fellowship of Christian Athletes meeting, Barker, the group's new leader, introduced speaker Wales Goebel to almost 100 athletes who packed the study hall room of Bryant Hall. The tall, lanky Goebel was still the captivating speaker that he had been for years as a youth evangelist. He told of his tough upbringing around bootlegging as a boy. He made everyone laugh about his courting days and meeting his Christian wife. It was a powerful message and at the end, he asked for all eyes to be closed.

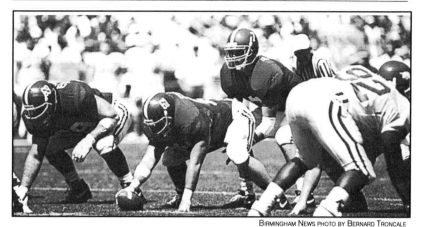

Barker takes snap from center Tobie Sheils against Arkansas; days earlier Sheils had been focus of attention at the weekly FCA meeting

He asked each player to ask themselves the question, "If you died tonight, are you sure you will go to Heaven?" He asked for those who wanted to be sure to lift their hand. Two athletes raised a hand. After a prayer, Goebel looked out at the group and said, "Now I want those two boys who raised their hands to come up here right now." Everyone looked around, wondering who the athletes were and whether they would come forth. Weaving their way through students sitting in study desks came senior co-captain Tobie Shiels, Alabama's All-SEC center, and Kevin Stephen, a track decathlete from Trinidad.

"Now Jay," Goebel continued as the two athletes stood facing the group, "I want you to come up here with your buddies...and pray that God will seal their commitment to the Lord."

Twenty players came forward, placed their hands on Tobie and Kevin as they knelt, and Barker prayed a moving prayer for his friends. As soon as the prayer was over, Barker was ecstatic. "That's my center! That's my center!" he exclaimed.

SATURDAY at Bryant-Denny Stadium, Alabama thrashed Arkansas 43-3 as Barker earned his 20th consecutive victory and, with it, the longest winning streak for a starting quarterback in Southeastern Conference history. Warren Rabb of LSU had 19 from 1957-59.

Louisiana Tech suffered a 56-3 loss to the Crimson Tide in Birmingham the following week. Barker left the game near the end of the first quarter with an abdomen pull, so Brian Burgdorf and Freddie Kitchens took over.

AT FCA that Wednesday night, the meeting format was for athletes to share what had been going on in their lives, good or not so good. Sophomore fullback Anthony Burroughs had been wanting to speak for some time, but just couldn't muster the courage before the group. But this particular night Burroughs stood in the back of the room.

"I'm kind of nervous as

BIRMINGHAM NEWS PHOTO BY FRANK COUCH

Barker plays well early against Louisiana Tech, but leaves the game with a stomach injury

you can see," Burroughs began. "I've always had a habit of cursing a lot. I don't mean to. It just comes out. I come to FCA meetings and I keep saying to myself that I'm going to quit.

"One night in the dorm, I was playing Nintendo and I let out a few curse words when Jay Barker walked by.

"Jay said something to me about my trash mouth in a nice way," he said, "and this time I really felt bad.

"I told Jay I was sorry and I said to myself, I'm not going to curse ever again.

"A little later that night at FCA, Jay handed me this scripture verse which says in James 1:26, 'If anyone considers himself religious and yet does not bridle his tongue, he deceives himself and his religion is worthless.' From that night on, which was about a year ago, I have stopped cursing. I can't say enough about how much guys like Jay, Matt (Wethington), Mickey (Conn), Roman (Colburn) and Chad (Key) have meant to me and my growth as a Christian."

The players broke into applause. Some high-fived Burroughs. A couple of them even hugged him.

THAT weekend, Alabama traveled to South Carolina to face a determined team of Gamecocks. Barker had recovered sufficiently from his stomach injury to go the distance for a 17-6 victory. He passed for 177 yards, completing 12 of 20 passes. It was Alabama's 28th consecutive victory, tying the school and SEC record, which also belonged to Bama in the late 70's.

Alabama took a week off before the Third Saturday in October showdown with Tennessee in Birmingham. Alabama was ranked second; Tennessee, tenth.

It would be the end of Alabama's winning streak, but the lingering public memory of Barker had more to do with a brilliant effort to push back seemingly certain defeat.

Down eight points at 17-9 with the ball on its own 17-yard line and 1:44 to play, Barker followed his offensive line to the ball. He set out on a miracle march by completing five passes in a row and six of nine overall in a drive to the one-foot line. Barker muscled the ball into the end zone himself on a sneak with 21 seconds left.

With no time-outs, he had called almost every play on the two-minute drill, covering 83 yards in 83 seconds.

After Barker got the final foot for six points, Stallings sent in David Palmer at quarterback, who took the ball from center, circled the right side and beat everybody to the end zone corner for two points and a 17-17 tie.

Barker was named ABC's Player of the Game, completing 22 of 40 passes for 312 yards, all career highs.

AGAINST Mississippi at Oxford the next week, Barker suffered another injury. A sprained shoulder mid-way the second quarter sent him to the sideline. Barker knew imme-

BIRMINGHAM NEWS PHOTO

Another injury, this time a shoulder, takes Barker out of the Mississippi game

diately it wasn't good. "The guy came right up the middle. We were trying to throw a screen, but Chris (Anderson) wasn't ready for the ball yet. I was up in the air when he hit me. I knew when it happened, I wouldn't be back," said Barker after the game. David Palmer played like a one-man team, taking over at quarterback in the third quarter. He passed for 54 yards, rushed for 38, caught eight passes for 76 yards, had 41 yards in punt returns and 34 in kickoff returns. Michael Proctor kicked four field goals of 46, 22, 53 and 49 yards as Alabama won a hard earned 19-14 victory.

STILL hurting from the injured shoulder, Barker shared a moment of humor and inspiration with his FCA buddies at their Wednesday meeting.

It was a letter that a South Carolina man had written to Barker.

The man told Jay that his son had obtained his autograph after the recently played South Carolina game in Columbia. "At first, we thought Rom. 8:28 under your autograph was your room number," he wrote.

"Then I realized it was a scripture verse. I hadn't read my Bible in quite a while, so I got it out and found Romans 8:28 (*And we know that all things work together for good to them that love God, to them who are the called according to his purpose*). I began to read other verses which led to more passages of scripture. As I read, the Lord began to convict me about my wife and I. We have been separated for some time. At this time, we are talking about getting back together and I just wanted you to know and thank you for the scripture verse when you signed your name for my son." You never know, Barker mused, how the Lord can use you. That fall Barker started a disciple-ship Bible study, teaching not only the Bible but also how fellow athletes can invest their lives in other men. "It was something taught to me by Dave Kemp, who was with Athletes In Action, and Shayne Kelley, who leads a Bible study with me and other players." That Bible study consists of Chad Goss, Lee Ferguson and Curtis Alexander.

BARKER and his injured shoulder sat out the homecoming game with Southern Mississippi, but he wasn't needed. Alabama triumphed 40-0.

The next Saturday brought a different story.

Alabama was ranked No. 5 in the nation with a 7-0-1 mark. LSU was not impressed. The Bengal Tigers brought their 3-5 record to Tuscaloosa, and stunned Alabama 17-13 to end the Crimson Tide's 31-game unbeaten streak. With the loss died Alabama's hopes of repeating as national champions.

Barker could only watch and wish that Stallings would send him into the fray so he could try to rally the team. Stallings would have no part of Barker's desire to play, however. "The thing that concerns us is that the trainer doesn't think he can take a good lick on that shoulder right now and I'm not going to play him."

DURING the time he was injured, Barker visited Tuscaloosa's Central

A recovering Barker rallies Alabama to victory against a tough Mississippi State team

West High School to talk to ninth and tenth graders. Some 175 students packed the room and 100 more stood outside to hear the quarterback.

"It wasn't long ago that I was in the ninth and tenth grades, and I know exactly the temptations you face everyday," Barker said. "But I want to encourage you today to stay away from beer and alcohol. Refuse drugs when offered to you. Keep you bodies pure. Abstain from sexual immorality... God want to bless your life and it's important that you choose the right kind of friends.

"Otherwise, you may have all the best intentions in the world, but one person can influence you in a negative way. Most of all, every person in here needs Jesus Christ to be the center of their life. I love Christ with all my heart and couldn't make it without him. I challenge you to allow Christ to be your Lord and Savior, and you'll see what a wonderful dif-

BIRMINGHAM NEWS PHOTO BY BERNARD TRONCALE

Barker squints into the sun as an Auburn defender closes in

ference He will make in your life as He has mine."

EVEN three weeks after Barker's injury, no one knew who Stallings would start at quarterback the following Saturday against Mississippi State in Tuscaloosa until David Palmer trotted onto the field for the first offensive possession.

On the third play, Palmer threw an interception that resulted in a 7-0 lead for State. Palmer took but two more snaps, and Stallings sent Barker in. The shoulder held, and he went the rest of the game. Palmer moved to receiver and ended up catching eight passes for 171 yards. Barker was back in form, completing 12 of 23 passes for 221 yards and a touchdown as Alabama notched a 36-25 victory.

Alabama had won three straight games over Auburn, two of them with Barker at the helm. The game was played at Auburn, but 48,000 people gathered in Bryant-Denny Stadium to watch a closed circuit viewing. With Auburn on probation, the game could not be televised on network TV. Barker was ready physically to start again and Alabama jumped to a 14-5 half-time lead and seemed in control. However, Auburn scored 17 points in the second half to take a 22-14 lead with 2:21 left in the game. Alabama was 73 yards from a touchdown and a two-point play to tie the game.

On the third play of the drive, Barker dropped to pass and was hit high and low. There was that sickening "pop" and amid the rising pain, Barker's left leg no longer responded correctly to the impulses of his brain.

This was Alabama's final drive of the game, and the crowd was on its feet. All but two. Barbara Barker and Jay's sweetheart Amy DiGiovanna remained in their seats. They had sat down prior to the injury to pray for the Lord to give Jay and his teammates peace in the final drive. It spared them both from seeing Barker crumble under the Auburn pass rush.

"In all his career, it was the only play of his that I ever remember missing," said Mrs. Barker. "I think the Lord kind of spared me on that one. We have it on tape, but I don't think I'm ever going to want to see it."

Barker had never before felt the grip of serious injury. But this time, a sheet of tough, fibrous tissue connecting bones around his knee had ripped. Doctors call it the anterior cruciate ligament. Only surgery would piece it back together. With that tear, Barker's season ended on the floor of Jordan-Hare Stadium.

Two teammates lifted Barker and carried him off the field. His friend and backup Brian Burgdorf came in and tried to save the game, but a fourth down pass fell incomplete.

Barker did not see the end. He had been carried immediately to the training room and listened to the conclusion on a radio. It was his first loss in 25 games as Alabama's starting quarterback.

Jerome and Barbara Barker waited anxiously outside the dressing room after the game. "God is going to use this for some reason. We just have to trust God. He has a plan in it all," said the quarterback as he joined them.

Later, he told the press, "This is just another challenge for me. I've been playing for 16 years since I was five and I've never been injured like this before. I've never had anything to keep me out."

The following Wednesday, the day before Thanksgiving, doctors at Healthsouth Medical Center in Birmingham spent two hours repairing the torn tissue.

Healthsouth is a place where the world's finest athletes come to have their bodies repaired. The skill of its surgeons is unsurpassed.

Even so, they can only piece together strands of tissue. It only gives the athlete a chance to start on the long, lonely, painful journey back to athletic form.

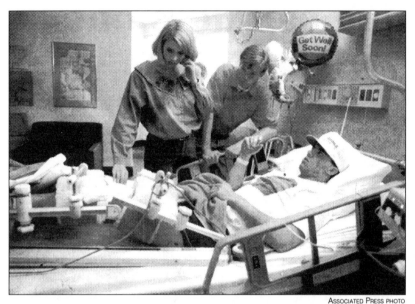

An elaborate brace system holds Barker's leg after surgery; girlfriend Amy DiGiovanna and her brother, Matthew, visit on Thanksgiving Day

On Thanksgiving morning he lay propped in his hospital bed, side rails up and left leg in a sling that elevated his left knee and, at the same time by a series of braces, held the leg immobile.

"Sitting around like this is as boring as can be," said Barker. "I'm going crazy."

Had the leg allowed, he would have been in therapy that moment.

"I want to be up and around and doing something," he said. "I sleep, eat, talk, watch TV and then sleep again."

Stallings came by, as did NASCAR driver Bobby Allison and Auburn quarterback Stan White, who also had been injured in the game.

Even in those first groggy hours after surgery, there was no question by anyone who knew Barker that he would return to form. "How bad can I feel?" he asked. "I've got a national championship and I'm 23-1-1 as a starter. That ain't all that bad."

And so he began the road back. First he had to stand. Then walk. Then bend and flex and add gradual stress to the damaged joint.

Days turned to weeks and weeks to months. Whatever the doctors and trainers asked, Barker accomplished.

"My family is so special and they couldn't do enough for me. It was difficult not to be up and around at first. My girl friend, Amy, was such a help to me after we got back to school, getting me to classes and places I had to go. She encouraged me when I wasn't feeling good and was always passing verses of scripture along to me. She made so many sacrifices that showed how much she cared for me."

WHEN Alabama met Florida for the second year in a row for the SEC championship game at Legion Field, Barker had no choice but to watch the game with Amy in Tuscaloosa. Florida won 28-13. Barker was more mobile for the Gator Bowl matchup with North Carolina in Jacksonville. He was on the sideline to watch Burgdorf's fine performance that earned MVP honors, and a 24-10 victory. Alabama's record was 9-3-1. In nine games, Barker had 1,525 yards passing, connecting on .573 percent of his passes.

FOR nine months after the surgery, the Alabama training room became a second home for Barker. Head Trainer Bill McDonald assigned Jimmy Rider, a man just a few years older than Barker, to work with Barker every morning and every afternoon.

First the muscles in his left leg were stimulated electrically, then he would go through a series of flexing and extending exercises.

From there he moved to a machine that moved his knee through a range of motions, with the machine doing the motions for Barker.

A series of stretching and flexing exercises followed, then the leg was iced down to keep it from swelling and getting sore.

He went through the drill five days a week, twice each day, an hour and a half each time.

Later, as the leg strengthened, exercises to improve the leg's range of motion moved to the pool, then later progressed to quad sets and straight leg raises.

The first strength-building drills began with a series of exercises just to help Barker's body maintain balance. There was the slant board, balance board, sliding board and finally boxes which he would jump on and off sideways.

Leg lifts continued with pressure gradually applied as the leg grew stronger.

Two months into rehabilitation, Barker began running in a swimming pool. First he ran with a flotation vest on, lifting his knees high, jogging, sprinting and then running backward. Later in the pool, Barker would go through the motions of throwing a pass.

Three months into treatment, Barker progressed to the practice field, going through the same drills that he had been going through in the pool. And so it went. Every week a little more resistance was added. Strength grew. Flexibility improved. Slowly. Slowly, the knee responded.

FACING his first major setback, Barker's faith took on a challenge different than anything he had ever experienced. "The injury was good for me because it brought back to reality my main purpose for living, and that is my relationship with the Lord," says Barker. "Because I had that knee injury, there resulted such a dependency upon God.

"I think sometimes, people need unmet needs in their life because if you don't have them, you can become self-righteous to the point of depending upon yourself for everything. I learned that people need to depend on Christ for every detail of their life through the good times and the bad. This really brought me into a more intimate relationship with God. People have so many doubts. Why did this happen to me, they say. Yet as I continued to trust Him, I realized what I saw as a trial, was truly a blessing in God's eyes. He was molding and making me into what he wants me to be."

McDonald had other insights about Barker in the rehabilitation process. "I think Jay matured a lot. He learned new things about himself. He learned a lot about discomfort, about pushing himself and making sacrifices he had to make in order to get himself ready to play again. It was a great learning experience for Jay as it usually is for most rehabilitation people. They usually go one of two different ways. They either begin to feel sorry for themselves in their rehabilitation or they start to learn about themselves and get better in their rehabilitation. I think the latter was true of Jay.

"After he got over the initial feeling of denial, disbelief, rejection and all of those things that all rehab people go through, regardless of what anybody else did, it was basically up to him to do the work to get back to where he wanted to be and beyond. It took a lot of his time but the fruits of his labor paid off," says McDonald.

As the 1994 football season approached, Barker looked toward his senior year with a perspective rare among players who have shared such a position in big-time college football.

"The greatest thing the Lord taught me is what's important in life. Football is not the most important thing in life. It's investing my life in people and realizing that the things God has to offer are eternal. The things the world has to offer through football or whatever are temporary."

Yet, perhaps his finest hour on the gridiron lay just ahead.

A fully-recovered Barker is prepared to quarterback the Crimson Tide as the 1994 season opens

FULL
RECOVERY

*I*nvitations to speak at churches, schools, youth rallies and community gatherings stacked up in Barker's mailbox.

Amid the invitations were letters from strangers, thanking him for his Christian and moral stand.

If America's youth had been looking for a role model, they had found it.

One request for an appearance came from the national FCA office. They wanted him as their speaker at the 1994 Super Bowl FCA Breakfast in Atlanta. He would share the platform with Coach Joe Gibbs, the former Washington Redskins coach.

Jay was excited as he and his dad drove to Atlanta for the Friday morning breakfast. The reservations list grew to 6,000. Most of the crowd ate their Chick-Fil-A box breakfasts in the stands of the Georgia Tech Arena, since the floor didn't come close to accommodating the audience.

Jay stood before that throng of young people and told them about his relationship with Christ, and gave his views against alcohol, drugs and sexual immorality. He had ten minutes. Gibbs, known as an eloquent speaker, followed.

Afterwards, a group gathered around the former Super Bowl coach for his autograph.

For Barker, the line of autograph seekers spread out before him, finally forming into a line that snaked around the halls of the arena. He signed autographs until 2 in the afternoon.

He signed every autograph that he could because it gave him the chance to write Rom. 8:28 beneath his name. For Barker, every autograph was a witness.

BARKER was equally faithful in his daily rehabilitation work and did what he could in the weight room as the other players sweated out winter conditioning workouts. Spring training rolled around in March and Stallings announced that Barker was making progress. Barker would wear a knee brace during spring practice, and contact work would be out of the question.

The offense took on a new complexion when Homer Smith replaced Mal Moore as offensive coordinator in January. Barker and Smith met for the first time at lunch in Bryant Hall on the day the new coach arrived from UCLA.

Barker had been fond of Mal Moore, and he knew that Smith had been on the Alabama staff during the time that Alabama had decided not to recruit him.

But now Moore was out of the picture, having moved to an administrative post, and here was Smith, the renown offensive genius from the staff that has passed Barker by.

But the issue was out of Barker's control, and now they sat together, sharing lunch and setting a tone for the year to come.

"Coach Smith was right up front with me from the beginning," said Barker. "He said, 'The reason we didn't recruit you was because we had already committed to more experienced high school quarterbacks at mid-season.' All of them were from out of state.

I just appreciated Coach Smith saying that to me from the start and after that, the issue was cleared up."

BARKER continued to speak to youth and church groups as time allowed. The mailbox was always filled with requests. One pastor of a large church said, "I'd rather have Jay Barker speak in my church than the hottest evangelist in the Southern Baptist Convention." On the Sunday following the A-Day game on April 17, Barker spoke on Friends Day for three morning services at First Baptist Church in Montgomery. One service was televised live in the Montgomery area and on cable TV the following week.

In June he was at the FCA's national conference at Black Mountain, North Carolina, where several hundred athletes and coaches gather each year.

On that sultry summer evening, all 650 conferees packed the College Hall assembly. The spot of featured speaker normally is reserved for professional athletes and college coaches. But on this night it was Barker.

Dressed in t-shirt, shorts, sneakers and with Bible in hand, Barker seized the opportunity for the next 23 minutes. He paced back and forth across the stage, like a young evangelist, quoting scripture, and encouraging his audience to success as an athlete and in life by trusting in what the Bible he was holding said.

After the assembly, Barker remained to lead a group on "Sex and Dating." Most of the session involved questions from the high school athletes. Barker was drilled for an hour on why he believed in sexual abstinence outside marriage. One boy asked, "How far should you go on a date?" Barker promptly answered, "From the neck up."

The next morning before Barker had to depart, he asked to hear Anne Graham Lotz speak to a group of coaches wives gathered at the conference. Anne, whose features resemble those of her famous father, Rev. Billy Graham, was easily recognized amid the group. But then, so was Barker as he stood, hoping not to be noticed, in the back of the room.

Anne spotted Barker and thanked him for his talk the previous evening, his love for Christ and the role model he was to young people. "And you know Jay," Anne said smiling and gesturing toward the other women present, "We all want you to marry our daughters and I have two!" Laughter filled the room and Barker might have blushed just a little.

PRE-SEASON football practice began, and Barker reported that his left knee—the injured knee—was stronger than his right one. He had done everything possible over the past nine months to be ready for his senior season.

There is always a fear that looms when an athlete tests a reconstructed knee for the first time. But when drills began, Barker pushed past the fear and fought for his job.

Burgdorf had been the Gator Bowl most valuable player, and had looked strong in spring drills.

Through two-a-day practices, Barker passed the test of contact in scrimmages and by the first game against Tennessee-Chattanooga, he had won the starting role.

In the first game, Alabama manhandled Chattanooga as expected, 42-13. Barker didn't play long, but was obviously sharp. In the next three games, the Tide squeaked by Vanderbilt 17-7 in Tuscaloosa, Arkansas 13-6 in Fayetteville and Tulane 20-10 in Birmingham. Alabama faithful and the media found the close scores hard to understand when Florida, Nebraska, Penn State and other powers were scoring 50, 60 and 70 points in some of their games. The defense was impressive but the offense wasn't scoring a lot of points. The offensive unit drew questions and criticism.

Alabama was winning but not impressively enough.

ALABAMA got by Arkansas the next week, but had trailed the Razorbacks 6-3 late in the third quarter before pulling ahead. Afterwards, Smith outlined what he saw as the problem: "Simplification is indicated. I started thinking that on Wednesday. I imposed a little too much (offensive scheme). And eventually, we will do more. But we don't have to have it all ready in any given week. We need to have Jay throw corner and post routes. We have to simplify Jay's passes and not worry about offensive design. And get the ball deep when it's there. That's what this athlete can do. When needed, the offense will be ready."

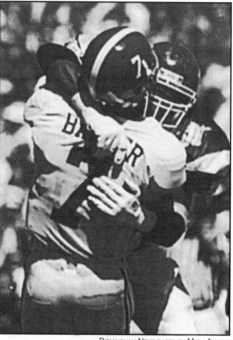

Arkansas tackler smothers Barker; early victories were hard earned

Two weeks later, Smith proved his genius.

Alabama fell behind Georgia 21-7 in the second quarter and appeared doomed. It was then that Barker was cut loose in the passing game and before the night was over had thrown for 396 yards, completing 26 of 34 passes. The 29-28 victory went down as one of Alabama's greatest comebacks. The offense had produced when needed and Barker suddenly felt pressure lifted. The performance had earned him Player of the Week honors by Sports Illustrated.

With a 5-0 record, Alabama was ranked 11th in both the AP and USA Today/CNN Coaches polls.

IN the homecoming game the following Saturday against Southern Mississippi, Barker was knocked out of the game with 13 minutes left in the third quarter with a badly bruised right shoulder. Before going to the bench, he had thrown a 45-yard pass to Patrick Hape, a 10-yard TD pass to Curtis Brown, and set an Alabama record with 100 passes without an interception. When he departed, Alabama led 14-

BIRMINGHAM NEWS PHOTO BY BERNARD TRONCALE

Barker suffers alone on sideline after being knocked out of Southern Miss game with a badly bruised shoulder

6, which turned out to be the final score. Homer Smith said after the game, "Burgdorf (who took over for Barker) has played brilliantly at times and is universally respected by the team. Buy Jay is Jay. He's our leader. He's sitting on a table in there being evaluated." Barker had an MRI the next morning and shoulder rehabilitation began immediately. Tennessee was just ahead.

Through six games, Barker's knee gave him virtually no problems. But now the shoulder injury. "As I sat in the stands and watched Jay play coming off his knee surgery, I would just pray, Lord, I know you love him more than I do, take care of him. And the Lord gave me peace," said Barbara Barker.

OFF the field, Jay continued to lead the FCA meetings each Wednesday night at 9 along with co-leader Matt Wethington. Meetings had to be moved across the street this fall from Bryant Hall to the Baptist Student Center. Crowds increased in the larger facility.

By the third meeting of the season, more than 160 student-athletes showed up to hear Clebe McClary, a Vietnam Marine hero and travels throughout the country as one of the FCA's most popular speakers.

The McClary visit was a highlight, but it was not a one-time crowd. Under Barker's leadership students from up to 70 miles away were attending the meetings.

It did not go unnoticed the attention and encouragement that Barker showed each person attending, no matter that person's sport or how highly (or lowly) that person might be ranked.

Another duty that went with the office involved the on-field post-game prayer that has become a part of every Alabama football game. Howard Cross, a former Alabama tight end who now plays for the New York Giants, started the post-game prayer in 1987. Since then the practice has been taken up by a number of players across America.

At Alabama, this year it was Barker's responsibility to rally players of both teams together for prayer.

IN spite of the sore shoulder, Barker said he was ready to play against the Vols. Neyland Stadium contained 96,856 spectators, most of them faithful to the home team which this year was favored to win by four points.

Ignoring the pain of a still-sore shoulder, Barker led the Tide to a come-from-behind win in Knoxville

Nevertheless, Tennessee still couldn't find a way to beat Alabama. It was 3-3 at the half and 10-10 at the end of three quarters, Alabama's touchdown coming when Barker hit Marcel West over the middle for 29 yards.

But with 7:45 remaining in the game, Tennessee had regained the lead 13-10. Alabama had first down at its own 20.

Five minutes later, Barker had directed an 80-yard march in 13 plays in what Smith called "the greatest drive of my life. It was a great job by the coaching staff—the play-calling was a committee effort—and a great job by the players." Barker rolled out and hit Curtis Brown on a crucial fourth and eight play at the Vols 40 for a first down to keep the drive going. His option pitch to Tarrant Lynch for 16 yards with a punishing block from Chad Key, got the ball to the four where Sherman Williams scored. Then, Alabama's defense stopped the Vols at Bama's seven yard line to save the 17-13 victory.

"I think Jay Barker was the difference." said Tennessee coach Phillip Fulmer afterwards. "His ability as a play maker...his ability to make things happen was the difference."

What started spectacularly with Georgia was completed by Fulmer's assessment. If in fact Jay Barker had ever been a caretaker quarterback, that was past.

This was his time. He was the play maker. Whatever

BIRMINGHAM NEWS PHOTO BY FRANK COUCH

Stallings passes instructions to Barker, who led Alabama to victory over Mississippi from a 10-point deficit

success Alabama was to have down the stretch would be on his shoulders.

THE Tennessee win was a confidence builder for the 7-0 Tide, now ranked sixth by the coaches poll. But next game against Mississippi in Tuscaloosa almost turned into a disaster. Ole Miss had the home crowd in shock with a 10-0 half-time lead. However, some of Mississippi's momentum died in the second quarter when severe lightning forced both teams to their locker rooms for a 26-minute delay.

Alabama settled in the second half with the defense shutting the Rebels down and Barker directing drives of 71 and 53 yards that put Alabama in the lead. On the go-ahead touchdown, Barker rolled and fought his way into the end zone from a yard out for the only touchdown of his career in Bryant-Denny Stadium.

BARKER was now 31-1-1, having moved past the record of the great Harry Gilmer who had a 30-9-2 record in 1944-47. "It feels really good to finally get the record," Barker said. "I thank God to be surrounded by a good team.... I feel really blessed that I've been surrounded by the teammates I've had. It means a lot to me, but it's not just me. It's the 10 other guys on offense and the ll guys on defense that made this all possible through all these games."

WITH an 8-0 record, the team finally got a week off, but it was to be a special weekend for Barker, nonetheless. That Friday night, 6,000 spectators crowded into 3,000 seats at Hewitt-Trussville High School stadium to witness the retirement of jersey number 11.

"Jay was one of the top athletes to ever play at Hewitt," said Barker's football coach Jack Wood, who is still the school's coach. "But the reason we wanted to honor Jay was because of his character, his role model to young people as a devout Christian, and all he has meant to this high school while he was here and now at Alabama. He has been such an inspiration. He conducts himself the way all of us should." Barker received proclamations from the Trussville City Council, Jefferson County Board of Education and the Jefferson County Commission.

"It means a lot to me and I feel so honored, but I can't take credit for it," said Barker. "I think of it as an honor for the people who got me to this point, everybody from my Little League coaches who helped me develop to my parents and the friends I've been around who helped make me a better person. I want kids to look at my life and the relationship I have with the Lord. I'm...not overbearing. But I try to live it the best I can. I don't mind if people recognize me for that more than just being a football player."

EIGHT nights later before a crowd of 75,453 in Tiger Stadium at LSU, Barker's third pass completion to Toderick Malone made him Alabama's all-time leading passer. This was one game Alabama didn't have to come from behind to win. They were ahead 28 to 3 at the half. Barker passed for 130 yards on six of 11 passes, the biggest a 59-yard TD connection with Curtis Brown just before the half.

Barker had gone eight games and 155 passes without an interception but his streak ended at 156 in the first half. The final score was 35-17 and it marked Alabama 700th all-time win. Bama was now 9-0 and ranked 4th by the USA Today/CNN coaches poll and sixth by AP.

ALABAMA fans feared Mississippi State and Coach Jackie Sherrill the next week at Starkville. State still had a chance to win the SEC West Division and they were hungry for the opportunity. They came into the game having won four in a row and six of their last seven games. The Bulldogs took charge quickly and held a 14-3 margin with 2:10 left in the half. Then Barker rallied the offense with a 74 yard drive in six plays to narrow the score to 14-9 at half-time. In the drive, Barker hit Brown for 44 yards, Malone for 26 on third and nine, and capped it off with a two-yard TD toss to Sherman Williams.

But the real fireworks would wait until the fourth quarter.

With 7:57 left in the game, Alabama was down 25-15. That is when, as Toderick Malone explained, "Jay took over." From his 35, Barker was sacked for a seven yard loss. Then he hit West for 18 yards, Brown for 9 and then a bomb to Brown for 42 yards and a touchdown. The drive took seven plays and used 2:37.

Alabama forced State to punt and got the ball back on its 35 with 3:41 left. Alabama trailed 25-22. Barker threw to Brown for 11 yards and to Tarrant Lynch for 11 more. Then Barker scrambled before tossing to Sherman Williams who made a circus catch for 28-yards down the right sideline. Five running plays later, Dennis Riddle lowered his head behind Lynch for the final yard at left end. 51 seconds remained.

When it was over, Barker had thrown for 325 yards and three touchdowns, hitting 26 of 35 passes (11 straight at one point for a school record). "It was a living, breathing Jay Barker that brought the Tide back from the dead," wrote Cecil Hurt of the *Tuscaloosa News*. "The charm is clearly upon the Tide, as personified by the amazing Jay Barker. If the Heisman Trophy is construed as going to the 'best' player, in terms of physical talent, he may not deserve it; if it is awarded to the 'most valuable' player, then it ought to be crated up and shipped to Tuscaloosa without further delay."

Receiver Curtis Brown, who had eight catches for 153 yards, said, "Jay is the type of quarterback who can get the job done whenever it has to be done." Smith too spoke with pride about his quarterback. "If Jay Barker played for personal self-aggrandizement, as many quarterbacks do at this stage in their career, then his teammates would not be 10-0 at this point. There are a lot of guys whose teams win, and you say they are winners, and that's fine. But Jay Barker makes his team win, and that is the difference. He's really what a quarterback should be. Jay Barker is a quintessential college leader quarterback. He plays within the means of the moment."

Mississippi State coach Jackie Sherrill offered even stronger remarks. "There is no question that the difference in the game was number 7.

"I've seen a lot of college quarterbacks, but I've never seen anyone as good as number 7," said Sherrill. "He's probably the best quarterback I've seen. It's the same thing every game. You go back and look at every game he's played in and it's the same thing. They'll win the games. They wouldn't have won their last three games without number 7."

Barker's game against Mississippi State impressed Bulldogs linebacker Scott Gumina to say, "As far as I'm concerned, he's (Barker) a Heisman Trophy winner." USA Today that same week included Jay in its Heisman Watch for the first time.

ESPN'S crew of Chris Fowler, Lee Corso and Craig James set up for live coverage on the day of the Alabama-Auburn game the following Saturday at Legion Field. "It's the Game of the Year," said Corso. The three anchormen along with game announcers Ron Franklin and Mike Gottfried had been twittering about Barker's play ever since the Georgia game. After the LSU game Gottfried had gone so far as to say that Jay had become his choice for the Heisman Trophy.

Barker would not disappoint. His fire power from the last eight minutes of the Mississippi State game would carry over, and for the Alabama faithful it would be a good thing.

Terry Bowden's Auburn Tiger team had not lost a game in its last 21 starts. Only a 23-23 tie with Georgia the previous week kept the state from seeing its two highly ranked teams meet undefeated.

On Tuesday during preparation week, Stallings held Barker out at practice as an example of his hard work and what he had accomplished, something Coach Bryant did in his coaching days to recognize leadership. "That's a guy who worked and worked and worked and now he's going to break every record at Alabama," Stallings said after practice. "He made it happen. He ought to be an inspiration to everybody who wants to get better."

ALABAMA was in command from the start before a Legion Field crowd of 83,091 and 700 members of the media from across the nation. The first Bama touchdown came when Sam Shade recovered an Auburn fumble at the Tide 47. In eight plays, Sherman Williams scored from the 13 with 2:38 remaining in the first quarter. Barker threw two third down passes—to Curtis Brown for 11 yards and 13 more to Tarrant Lynch to spark the drive. Immediately afterwards, Alabama forced Auburn to punt. Backed to the 26-yard line on first and 15, Coach Woody McCorvey sent a play to the huddle that called on a combination of quarterback judgment, accuracy and strength.

Barker fired a long pass to Toderick Malone over the middle, dead on the money. Malone wound his way down field for a spectacular 74-yard touchdown catch and run as the first quarter ended. Alabama was up 14-0.

Five minutes later, Barker and his troops struck again. Starting on their own 13, a reverse to Chad Key resulted in him dropping the ball, recovering and whipping a pass to Barker, mainly to avoid a safety but resulting in an 11-yard gain and first down. Williams, who had 164 yards rushing for the day, got 14. Then Barker dropped back and hit a streaking Marcel West on a post pattern over the middle that covered 49 yards to the end zone. The 21-0 lead at half-time was a shock to both Alabama and Auburn fans. Such dramatics had occurred for Alabama, mostly in desperation in fourth quarters throughout the season. "We got our halves mixed up," Stallings joked afterwards.

Auburn came back hard in the second half and Alabama

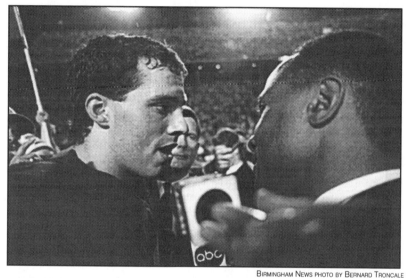

BIRMINGHAM NEWS PHOTO BY BERNARD TRONCALE

ABC sideline announcer Lynn Swann grabs Barker for comments after the Auburn win

held on for a 21-14 win.

Alabama's offensive line, maligned much of the season for spotty pass protection and narrow running lanes, gave perhaps its best performance of the year. Jon Stevenson, Joey Harville, Kareem McNeal, Maurice Belser, John Causey, Will Friend, Jeremy Pennington, Pete DiMario and Laron White gave coaches Jim Fuller and Danny Pearman cause to smile. They also gave Barker time to roll up 177 yards passing, completing 8 of 17 throws and two touchdowns.

As the game ended, Barker sprinted toward the Auburn sideline and the man who had helped him develop quarterback skills in two years of summer football camp. Barker and Auburn Coach Terry Bowden embraced in a bear hug.

"I've known Jay since high school," Bowden would say a little later. "He had a great game today. I hope Auburn fans know how much I wanted to win the game. But I love Jay Barker."

THEN Barker raises his right hand to gather teammates and Auburn players at the center of the field for a prayer. Jay kneels in the center of a mob of players and takes the hand of Auburn quarterback Patrick Nix in one hand and Auburn receiver Frank Sanders with his other hand. Praying loud to be heard, Barker thanked God for their ability to perform together and to glorify his name on the field of play. He asked the Lord to quickly heal any players who may have been injured. Then he asked God to bless the Auburn program; "even though we play on different teams," he said, "we are on the same team together in Christ."

Inside the dressing room, coaches and writers were reflecting on accomplishments of the just completed season.

Barker and the other Alabama seniors had just notched their 44th victory, tying the school record for a senior class.

For the Auburn game, Barker had completed 8 of 17 passes, two for touchdowns, and one interception. He even caught an ll-yard pass from Chad Key.

He also surpassed Scott Hunter for career attempts (689) and completions (392). His 920 career plays moved him ahead of the record (904) held by Walter Lewis. "You just can't imagine what Jay has meant to this football team," said

Stallings after the game. "He's 34-1-1 as a starter. I don't know if that will ever be equaled."

He still had not lost a game that he finished.

The team was 11-0 and polls placed Alabama third in the nation. Its third consecutive Southeastern Conference championship game with Florida awaited in Atlanta.

Against LSU, Jay Barker became the all-time passing leader in the 102-year history of Alabama football

PASSING ALL OTHERS

*H*ow many men have thrown a pass in the 102-year history of University of Alabama football? A hundred? Two hundred?

Pat Trammell. Richard Todd. Harry Gilmer. Dixie Howell. Jeff and Gary Rutledge. Steve Sloan. Kenny Stabler. Joe Namath.

As with all competition, only one can have thrown for more yardage than all the others.

Jay Barker became that man November 5, 1994, on the floor of Tiger Stadium during a game in which the University of Alabama defeated Louisiana State University 35-17.

TO accomplish such a deed that outdistances all others in a century of trying deserves a special accounting.

This is not, however, a recitation of how Barker came to that special day. Rather, it is a dissection of the day, a glimpse inside the routines and habits that football men practice before each competition.

Friday, November 4

8 a.m. - Barker eats breakfast with Chad Summers at the Waffle House. Summers was a wide receiver for Barker in high school, and is now a student at Alabama and leads the singing at the Alabama Fellowship of Christian Athletes meetings.

10 a.m. - The Marketing 313 class has been canceled, so Barker has quiet time in his room, packs for the trip to Baton Rouge and gets dressed for travel.

11:30 a.m. - Barker grabs lunch in the Bryant Hall dining room.

12:30 p.m. - Players begin piling into three buses that are parked at the front of Bryant Hall. A police escort idles nearby to lead the entourage to the Tuscaloosa airport. Barker strides to the bus in blue blazer, khaki slacks, white shirt and red tie decorated with football player drawings. Travel bag thrown over one shoulder, Barker pauses among well-wishers to sign autographs.

1 p.m. - Two grade school classes are waiting at the airport and want to see Barker and Stallings. Barker goes over, greets the children, then moves on to board the plane.

Player seating is by position. Jay is in 18A on an aisle and Lance Tucker and Freddie Kitchens share the seat row with him. Cups of ice are distributed. Three cans of juice and soft drink are in the seat pockets for each player. Also at each seat is a sack lunch of turkey and roast beef sandwiches, potato chips, cheese and crackers, apple, king size Reese's candy and two chocolate chip cookies. Stewardesses pass out packages of peanuts and pretzels as the players dig into the lunch bags.

The 45-minute flight is uneventful. Frozen ice cream cones are distributed. The plane bounces on the landing, drawing plenty of player commentary. Players always antici-pate how well the landings go and often applaud when it's a smooth one.

2 p.m. - Victory Bus Lines of Tuscaloosa has four buses waiting. They follow a police escort to Holiday Inn-South. Players get room assignments and keys. Barker is in 224 with roommate Brian Burgdorf. Players room by position.

3 p.m. - The team boards the Victory buses for Tiger Stadium and an abbreviated Friday afternoon practice. Players go straight to the visitor locker room. First timers are surprised at how small it is, and, according to those who claim to know, that is remains the same as it was 40 years ago. A sign indicates that it will be enlarged after the season. Barker's locker is next to the door leading to the stadium.

3:45 p.m. - The team takes the field. It is 81 degrees, balmy for November. Barker starts throwing soft passes. The players are whistled together by Stallings to begin the tune-up for Saturday's game.

Ron Franklin, Mike Gottfried and Mike Adamle of ESPN visit to pick up tidbits to use in their broadcast.

4:30 p.m. - The team boards the buses and the police escort them through Friday afternoon Baton Rouge rush hour traffic.

6 p.m. - Dinner is served in a large dining room off the Holiday Inn lobby. Head Trainer Bill McDonald has ordered steak and chicken, spaghetti, baked potatoes, vegetables, bread, tea and soft drinks. No desserts. Like every Friday night team meal, Tarrant Lynch sits to Barker's left and Mickey Conn to his right. Roman Colburn and Matt Wethington are in the mix. Joining the group this year is John David Phillips. "We always eat every meal together on game weekends," says Barker.

6:45 p.m. - The team is in the buses again, for a ten-minute ride to a movie theater. Jumbo buckets of popcorn and large cokes are waiting for the players to pick up as they file into the theater. Movie goers are flabbergasted at first. Some recognize the Alabama team and some do not. After buying a package of M&M's, Barker takes his usual end row seat to the left wall on the next to last row. He saves a seat for Lance Tucker and Assistant Trainer Jimmy Rider. "We always sit together at the movies," say Barker. The team shares the movie with other viewers who were there to see "Stargate." Coach and Mrs. Stallings, son, John, and daughter, Martha Kate, along with Gerald Jack have joined the team and sit on the back row.

9:15 p.m. - The team buses back to the motel and goes directly to a meeting room off the lobby. For 20 minutes, Stallings talks his squad through a detailed overview of what to expect from LSU. Walking back and forth in red blazer and speaking in a low tone, Stallings covers detail after detail, every tendency of the opponent and every situation to expect without a note in his hand. "You should be able to write a page on the man you are going to face tomorrow. If you can't, you are not prepared," he said. Barker sat in the middle of the front row and Stallings focused on him: "Jay should be able to tell you who their weakest cornerback is and who their strongest cornerback is. If he can't, he is not prepared." He spoke to other individuals. Players broke into offensive and defensive meetings for another 20 minutes and it was over.

10:15 p.m. - Snack time. Pizza, soft drinks, fruit, ice cream, nuts and toppings. Barker has a quick snack and heads to his room.

Saturday, November 5

7 a.m. - Balmy sunshine has been replaced by rain.

8 a.m. - A man in jeans, sneakers and crimson jersey with the number 7 on the front and back steps out of the Holiday Inn and yells, "Roll Tide!"

9 a.m. - Players get wake-up calls.

10 a.m. - The lobby is filled with fans crowding in to see Alabama players come down for breakfast. One woman asks,

"Has Jay Barker come by yet?" She held a camera and wanted to take a photograph of Barker posed with her husband, who stood nearby wearing a red cap with a stuffed gray elephant on top. When Barker arrives, the crowd pushes toward him with scraps of paper in hopes of an autograph. Camera shutters clicked. Barker gestures to each person as he slides in with the players toward the dining room. McDonald has ordered breakfast steak, waffles, eggs, grits, potatoes, sweet rolls, milk and orange juice. Barker and his table regulars sit at the same table, in the same seats as they did for dinner the night before.

10:30 a.m. - Players go into the kicking meeting and position group sessions for a half hour. Heavy rain falls

11:30 a.m. - Players rest in their rooms and watch the Miami-Syracuse and Arkansas-Mississippi State games on television.

2:30 p.m. - The pre-game meal is baked chicken, potatoes and vegetables and bread. The players eat quietly.

3 p.m. - Mickey Conn, Roman Colburn and Chad Key join Brian Burgdorf and Barker in his room for devotion and prayer.

4 p.m. - The team boards Victory Lines buses for Tiger Stadium. Barker takes his usual second row seat behind the driver of the first bus. His seatmate is Freddie Kitchens. "We always sit together on the bus at that same spot," says Barker.

4:30 p.m. - Close to 2,000 Alabama fans wait at the entrance gate to greet the players. The players go through the dressing room where Equipment Manager Tank Conerly and his crew have the white road uniforms and pads hanging at each locker. At each station is a game program. Moving through the dressing room, the team takes its traditional stroll across the playing field to the far end of the stadium and back. Barker walks with Burgdorf, looking up to see only Boy Scouts and ushers in place. The smell of steaming hot dogs wafts across the field.

4:50 p.m. - Barker leans back on a training room table and gives Jimmy Rider a good angle to tape his ankles.

5 p.m. - Stallings sits alone on a bench outside the dressing room underneath the stadium.

5:30 p.m. - Kickers, quarterbacks and receivers come out to warm up under the lights.

6:32 p.m. - An official escorts Barker and co-captains Tarrant Lynch, Tommy Johnson and Sam Shade from the dressing room tunnel for the pre-game coin toss. The scouts and ushers now have been joined by 75,453 other people. The coin was tossed and Barker called 'heads.' It was 'tails.' LSU defers its choice to the second half and Alabama takes the ball. Barker and his teammates shake hands with the LSU captains, and as they turned to trot back to their respective sidelines, someone grabs Barker's hand. It was one of LSU's honorary captains, a member of the 1969 team which last beat Alabama in Baton Rouge. "I just want to thank you," he said, "for your Christian witness."

6:37 p.m. - Marcel West returns the opening kickoff to the 10-yard line. Barker needs 24 yards to become Alabama's all-time leading passer. On the third play, he hits Toderick Malone for 9 yards. Alabama is forced to punt.

Alabama scores on the return of an LSU fumble and after kicking off stops the Tigers on downs.

On first down Barker throws to Curtis Brown for 11 yards to the Alabama 49. Barker then drops back, hits Malone across the middle for 28 yards. The record is his.

By half-time, Alabama is up 21-3.

Barker does not throw a pass in the second half, as Alabama cruises to a 35-17 victory.

Barker had another record of sorts that night; one that he would just have soon passed up. He threw his first interception of the year, ending his school record string at 155 throws. Jeff Rutledge and David Smith shared the previous record at

99.

On the sideline after the game, announcer Mike Adamle found Scott Hunter, the former Alabama quarterback who for the previous 24 years had held the Alabama passing record. "I can't think of a better or classier young man to break the record," he said, "than Jay Barker."

Birmingham News photo by Tom Self

Honors mounted for Barker as the 1994 season wound down, but none was more important than the respect of team members

HONORS
ROLL IN

*M*onday after the November 21 Auburn game, *USA Today* carried Barker's picture on the front page. It led into the Sports section lead headline "Alabama is now squarely in the (national) championship hunt."

In one interview, Barker was asked about Alabama's hopes for a national title, being third behind undefeated Nebraska and Penn State. "I feel like we've got a chance," he said. "We've just got to keep winning games. We've been talking about it ever since September. That's our goal. We'd like to be further up now than No. 3. If we're 13-0, we've done our job. Going 12-0 is hard. Try going 13-0 and playing the SEC Championship."

TUESDAY, the newspapers announced that Barker was running fourth in a Heisman Trophy tracking poll by the *Denver Post*. "It's kind of weird," said Barker. "You go from being criticized earlier in the year to being up for that. I truly mean it when I say that things like the Heisman Trophy are good, but it means more to me how the team does. I feel very proud about it and I feel very honored to be put up for it, but winning is what is most important to me." The poll had Jay behind Colorado's Rashaan Salaam, and Penn State's Kerry Collins and Ki-Jana Carter. If he had a vote, Jay said he would "probably vote for one of my linemen. My next vote would be (Tide running back) Sherman Williams."

Homer Smith was pleased by the attention Jay was suddenly receiving. "If they look carefully at him and make him a Heisman candidate, then I think more of the process. He is what a Heisman candidate should be. He is selfless and manages the team. He works hard at the game and puts something back into the company."

Suddenly, within the span of a half dozen football games, Barker was transformed from caretaker to play maker.

"I would like to see Jay Barker become a football coach," wrote *Birmingham News* columnist Clyde Bolton. "I think he would be a grand success. His Christian witness is important to him, and a coaching job would be a worthy outpost for exercising it. I've seen a lot of kamikaze tackles and suicide blocks this season, but Jay Barker performed the bravest act I've ever seen by a college football player. He told the press he was a 22-year-old virgin."

It seemed as though everyone had saved up praise for Barker until the end. And now it was time to let go.

After a Thanksgiving Day practice for the Florida game, Athletic Director Hootie Ingram and Stallings provided the team, coaches and families dinner in the Sheraton Capstone Inn. Afterwards, several went back to their rooms to watch ESPN's game between Syracuse and West Virginia. At half-time, the ESPN crew reviewed the season, talked about upcoming games, and gave a rundown on the Heisman candidates. When Beano Cook's turn came, he chose the Alabama quarterback as the target for one of his one-liners: "Jay Barker is the greatest winner in the South since Robert E. Lee."

ALABAMA players and coaches watched the Florida-Florida State game with great interest the following Saturday. Florida looked scary when they took a 31-3 lead into the fourth quarter over the Seminoles. But when the game was over, somehow Florida State had scored four touchdowns and the game ended in a 31-31 tie. Alabama knew it was in for another war with Florida, regardless of what happened in that fourth quarter.

On Monday of game week, Barker was named to the Associated Press All-Southeastern Conference team. It was the first time he had been chosen All-SEC in his Alabama career in spite of his starting record and national championship season.

On Wednesday, Scripps Howard News Service Heisman Poll had Barker in fifth place.

Friday morning at 7:30, a ringing phone shook Barker out of bed. It was Johnny Unitas. *The* Johnny Unitas. The greatest professional quarterback of his time. He was just calling to let Barker know that he had been selected for the Johnny Unitas Golden Arm Award, presented each year to the nation's top senior quarterback.

The Unitas banquet a week later in Louisville gave Barker time to enjoy the honor of the award. But on this Friday, everything would have to wait.

At 9:30, the team flew to Atlanta, dropped their bags at the Stouffer Concourse Hotel at the Atlanta airport, and bused to the Georgia Dome for an afternoon workout.

It did not take Stallings' constant reminders that even an 11-0 team does not go to the Sugar Bowl or play for the national championship except through the SEC Champion-

Barker passes for an early touchdown against the Gators

ship game.

Some 74,751 fans packed the stadium, even more than the Super Bowl drew in January.

On the third play of Alabama's first possession, Barker scrambled out of the pocket to his right and spotted Curtis Brown over the middle behind the defensive back. Barker rifled the ball to Brown who grabbed it and ran untouched for a 70-yard touchdown.

Florida quarterback Danny Wuerffel responded with a 72-yard Gator drive to tie the score at 7-7.

Barker came right back and marched the Tide inside the Florida 10, but a sack and an illegal procedure penalty forced Michael Proctor to kick a 22-yard field goal to put Alabama up 10-7.

Florida followed with a field goal. Later, a blocked punt cost Alabama a touchdown with 1:15 to go in the half. Florida led 17-10.

Florida may have been America's greatest offensive team in 1994. But it was a defensive play in the second quarter that perhaps had the most to do with Florida's success in this game.

Barker was dropping to pass when Gator Kevin Carter slammed him to the turf. Barker struggled to his feet and trotted off the field. His left arm hung limply at his side. The

The Florida defense sufficiently banged up Barker that his passing accuracy suffered

pain was obvious. On the next series, Barker was back, but his throwing motion seemed noticeably different. Suddenly, more passes were off target than on.

Working through the pain, after half-time Barker led the Tide into position for two third-quarter field goals by Proctor of 47 and 48 yards. And as the fourth quarter began the teams were separated by a single point, 17-16 Florida.

Midway through the fourth, Alabama freshman line-backer Dwayne Rudd intercepted a Wuerffel pass and ran it into the end zone from 23 yards out to put Alabama ahead 23-17. It looked like Alabama's come-from-behind magic was working again.

But this time it was not to be. Florida Coach Steve Spurrier orchestrating an 80-yard touchdown drive that put Florida back on top 24-23 with 5:29 left to play.

Barker and his offensive teammates tried desperately to get within field goal range. As Doug Segrest of *The Birmingham News* wrote, "Barker's string of miracles ended on a fourth-and-13 at the Alabama 44." His final pass, toward Toderick Malone, was tipped away and intercepted by Florida with 47 seconds left.

"I thought we'd pull it out again," said Barker, surrounded by reporters and cameramen after the game. "It was a hard fought game. We're upset we did not win the game, but we're going to get through this. We had some penalties kill some drives and that didn't help us, but we have so much to be comforted by and happy with. We've had a great season, and with a win in the bowl game, we could go 12-1."

It was a heartbreaking defeat, and a costly one for Alabama. A one point loss after an 11-0 season denied the team an SEC title, a Sugar Bowl appearance and a chance to meet Florida State for a shot at the national title. Instead they would meet Ohio State in Orlando's Citrus Bowl.

In spite of his shoulder injury, Barker had fought back through five sacks and managed to complete 10 of 19 passes for 181 yards, one touchdown and two interceptions. To that point, Barker had only three interceptions all season.

After the game, Jay knelt at the center of the field with Wuerffel and Carter, whose sack had sent Barker to the sideline, and a large group of other players from both teams.

How small the world must have seemed at that moment, as Wuerffel led the group in prayer. Three years earlier, Barker had been host to Wuerffel when Alabama was recruiting the Florida quarterback. And only six months earlier Barker, Wuerffel and Carter had together attended a Christian retreat for SEC athletes at Samford University. They had even been teammates in the retreat volleyball competition.

Feeling as much disappointment as any time in his playing career at Alabama, Barker left the prayer and ran to the dressing room with head up and helmet in hand. "When I went in, I realized that I needed to run off the field the same when I had lost, as I always did when I won. I wanted to give the appearance that it wasn't like I didn't try. I had fought a good battle and had given everything I had."

The dressing room was hushed. Stallings led the team in the Lord's Prayer, then tried to console his players by reminding them of the outstanding games they had played and the near-perfect record they had produced over the season.

Barker knelt by his locker and reached back to his faith for comfort. "You have to realize that there is a reason and purpose behind it. A lot of times we may not like it and we may not think it is in our best favor, but yet God is sovereign. He knows what is best for our lives. So I realized at that moment, that I just needed to bow my head and just humbly come before Him and thank Him for the loss. That may sound dumb to a non-Christian, but to a Christian that's what we should do because God will bring good out of it."

DURING the SEC championship game weekend, the Academic All-SEC team was announced. Barker was one of four Alabama players chosen.

BACK at Tuscaloosa, Barker had little time to reflect. First, he found a window of his black GMC Jimmy truck smashed. It had nothing to do with the game; it was just a simple break-in, easily fixed. The news got better fast. He was notified Sunday that he had been invited as a finalist to the Heisman Trophy presentation in New York City on Saturday evening. He was already scheduled for the ESPN College Football Awards Show in Orlando on Thursday night as a Davey O'Brien Outstanding College Quarterback finalist, and was scheduled for the Unitas banquet in Louisville Friday.

It was Dead Week on the Alabama campus. Final exams. Barker worked on a term paper and was granted an extension to finish it after his trip. Getting his trip organized and clothes laundered, Barker flew out of Birmingham on Wednesday morning for Orlando. The ESPN show would feature nine awards including the O'Brien, the Doak Walker Award, The Jim Thorpe Award, the Outland Trophy, the Maxwell Award, the Butkus Award and several others. Twenty of the nation's finest college players attended as finalists.

Barker was housed at the Beach Club Hotel at Disney World with the other athletes. He hung out with Eric Zeier of Georgia and Kerry Collins of Penn State. The trio found it amusing to mingle with the Disney World crowds and no one noticing who they were. "It's kind of feels funny just walking around and nobody comes up to you," said Barker. "It's kind of nice for a change."

Disney-MGM Studios was this year's site for the awards show.

Chris Fowler was emcee while Craig James and Lee Corso interviewed the athletes and passed out the awards. Barker was on the front middle row and Stallings, who flew in that day, sat beside him. The first award was the Davey O'Brien Award. Film highlights of Jay, Eric and Kerry were shown. Kerry was announced the winner, and Jay and Eric congratulated him on his way to the stage.

A little later in the show, Craig James joined the audience

and interviewed Barker and Zeier, sitting back to back to each other. James asked Barker about his hopes for pro football.

"I just want a chance to do what I've done at Alabama, to hopefully motivate guys to win. Eric and I were talking and we decided we would split Health Shuler's (former Tennessee QB, now with Washington Redskins) salary of six million dollars. If anyone wants a deal, Eric and I will come as a package for three million a year," Barker said to the roar of laughter from the studio audience.

Barker was also a candidate for the Maxwell Award, given to the nation's outstanding college player, as selected by that award's committee. Collins was a surprise winner. However, Barker learned that three of his votes for the award came from Auburn head coach Terry Bowden, athletic director David Housel and sports information director Kent Partridge.

THE next morning, Barker and Zeier grabbed bacon, egg and cheese croissant sandwiches at the airport before he was off again to meet his parents, sister Andrea and girlfriend Amy for another award banquet.

For the few hours he was in the air the whirlwind stopped and Barker could look out the window as the patchwork of brown and green southern countryside passed far below. So much had happened since those days of oversize shoulder pads at Center Point's Metro field. So much was still to come.

For a little while he reflected with a friend on the good times and bad; of the trials and triumphs, of the accomplishments and the might-have-beens, and the sometimes quirky, sometimes poignant and sometimes seemingly insignificant things that shaped his life.

A favorite Bible verse, Romans 8:28....the verse he signs with his autograph. "When I got the shoulder injury at the beginning of the 1991 season that kept me from having a chance to start, I clung to this verse...'And we know that all things work together for good to them that love God.' Later, I discovered that as people looked up Romans the eighth chapter and the 28th verse, they would flip back to the sixth chapter and to the third chapter where it speaks about salvation. So that was all the more reason to keep writing that scripture down, because people would discover other good passages in Romans.

ON publicity. "My dad told me when I came to Alabama to not read the newspapers and listen to talk shows. He said the quarterback gets too much credit and too much criticism. He said if you read a newspaper after a good game, you may think too much of yourself. If you read a newspaper after a poor game, you may think too little of yourself. So I just wait until after the season to read the newspapers.

COACH Mal Moore...Jay's position coach for four years. "He took me in like a father figure. He stood up for me many times when it wasn't his fault, especially when he had a young quarterback to work with. He always handled himself with such dignity and class. He knows so much about the game of football. I always respected him for being such a good family man too. I'm glad he was in my life and part of my life."

COACH Homer Smith...Jay's position coach as a senior. "He built confidence in me from day one. He complimented my playing before he got to Alabama. He knew everything about me. He cares so much for his quarterbacks and really loves the game of football. He has such a brilliant offensive mind and had coached so many great quarterbacks. He taught me so much about the quarterback position. I've been so blessed to have spent just this one year with him. I will remember and use things he taught me as long as I'm in football."

COACH Gene Stallings..."He taught me about being a competitor and hating to lose. He taught me how to work under pressure, and I now know that when he was hollering at me, he was trying to prepare me to play as quickly as possible in order to play early. The team takes on the personality of the head coach and he was very competitive and a classic guy off the field. He really impressed me by always going to the hospitals visiting people. He is so involved in the Rise Foundation for handicapped children and that all means a lot to the players, who have love and respect for him and that's why they want to win for him, too. He is just a great role model and with the wonderful family he has, it has given all the guys hope that good families are possible for them to have one day, too."

CHRISTIAN growth..."I have so many struggles. I hope people are not looking at me as a perfect guy because I'm not. A lot of people say, Jay you are so good and I say the only good in me is Jesus. And that's it. I still struggle with having a consistent quiet time. Too, I'm working on patience and ever since I was little, I've always had a temper. I've always asked God to help with that on and off the field. I think I've come a long ways in that area, but it just always came with my competitive spirit. I want to work on scripture memorization. I have a little box of scriptures and I try to learn a verse a week. That's the key to the Christian life because as Ephesians 6 says, the Word of God is the sword of the spirit. It pays to hide the Word in your heart. I'm still a long way from being where I want to be in that area."

FUTURE considerations..."Beyond wanting to be in pro

football, whatever I do I want to be in ministry regardless of the vocation. I think Christians should strive for good positions of influence and be as successful as possible. Then as they make a stand for Christ, their lives will have a greater impact for Him. I have thought about coaching and that interests me very much. Some of my buddies were talking the other night about coaching together some day. I'm just open to whichever direction the Lord leads me. I have thought about being a pastor, but I haven't felt that calling. If God allows me to do that, then I will be obedient to Him. But like I said, I feel like I have a call to ministry, to love God with all my heart and my neighbor as myself. Helping others through discipleship will always be important to me regardless of my occupation."

"...I'm working on patience and ever since I was little, I've always had a temper. I've...asked God to help me with that on and off the field. I think I've come a long way in that area, but it just came with my competitive spirit."

—Jay Barker

As with so many things, receiving the Unitas Award was a family affair for the Barkers. Joining Unitas from left, mom Barbara, sister Andrea, dad Jerome, fiancé Amy and Jay

EPILOGUE

HEISMAN FINALIST

*O*n the awning to the front entrance of the lower Manhattan building is a clean, simple brown sign: *Downtown Athletic Club*.

In smaller type on either side are the words *Home of the Heisman Trophy*.

Barker was there to join Kerry Collins, Ki-Jana Carter, Rashaan Salaam, Steve McNair and Warren Sapp to see who the 920 voters and 50 living past Heisman winners had selected as America's top collegiate football player for 1994.

The door opens and there it is, the original bronze Heisman Trophy on display in the lobby center. It has been there since 1935.

The building is what it says it is, an athletic club. The 35 floors house gyms, workout rooms, weight rooms, pools and courts for all types of athletic competition.

There is no 13th floor, however. That level is listed "H."

The elevator opens onto a brightly lit gallery. There are the portraits of the best of the best. Doc Blanchard. Glenn Davis. Doak Walker. Alan Ameche. Roger Staubach. John Cappelletti. Archie Griffin. Bo Jackson. Barry Sanders.

Working their way to assigned seats, the 1994 finalists listened as host Chris Fowler narrated highlights of each player's career.

There were shots of Barker completing passes, and Alabama winning games.

Gene Stallings stepped to a platform with Lee Corso and said, "The thing about Jay is that he just wants to win. He could care less if he completes a pass or not. He just wants to take the ball down the field and score. What a quality person Jay is and a role model that we really need today."

There was also a film clip made after the SEC championship game. In it, Florida defensive star Kevin Carter said Barker was his choice for the Heisman. "I don't think any player has exemplified the kind of leadership ability and has done as much for their team as Jay Barker in the last four years. He's probably the physically toughest I've faced. When you meet him, he shakes your hand and looks you right in the eye. He's somebody you can immediately respect."

It was the only interview of the night from an opposing player directed toward a finalist.

Barker took his turn at the back-of-the-room set with Craig James.

He was obviously pleased to be there, especially considering the road that a quarterback travels in the Alabama offensive system.

"I realized that at Alabama we were going to have a tough-nosed offense, and would not throw the ball as many times as most offenses do," he said. "We were going to be conservative, play good defense and because of that we won a national championship."

Barker went on to say that expectations are high at Alabama for quarterbacks because so many great ones have come from there.

James concluded the interview teasing Barker that "Lee Corso says you will be governor of Alabama some day," to which Barker replied, "I don't know about that. I'm not sure I want that responsibility."

Barker had been among the top half dozen candidates for the Heisman since November. He had never led the weekly Heisman watches.

So it was no surprise when Club president Francis H. Powers announced Salaam of Colorado as the 1994 winner.

Barker placed fifth in the final vote.

"It would have been exciting just to be here as a member of the audience," he said. "But to be here as a finalist is just really awesome to me."

At an autograph table after the presentation, Heisman executive director Rudy Riska came by to tell Barker and his parents that they would be coming back to New York in February.

"Street and Smith has selected you as the Exemplary Player of the Year for College Football." It goes annually to the player who has shown outstanding character and who has contributed the most to community service.

Back in Tuscaloosa the next week, it was as thought someone had turned on a spigot and forgot to turn it off.

The Birmingham News announced its All-SEC team and Barker was picked SEC Player of the Year.

The Nashville Banner announced that the SEC head coaches also had selected Barker Player of the Year in the SEC, with nine of the 12 voting for the Alabama quarterback.

"Considering I was coming back from a knee injury last season and the offense started so slowly, it means a lot to be recognized like this," said Barker. "Any time you're voted on by the coaches, it counts for something more because they're playing against you and they know what kind of player you are."

THE UNITAS AWARD

*A*t Louisville's historic Galt House fast against the Ohio River, Johnny Unitas found his first chance to meet Jay Barker. It is difficult to say who enjoyed it most.

It was Unitas' name that was on the award for America's top quarterback, and it was Barker's name on the winner's plaque.

The Kentucky Chapter of the National Football Foundation College Hall of Fame fed steaks to more than 800 that night.

Gene Stallings was there, leading an Alabama contingent that included Homer Smith and Mal Moore, his administrative assistant Gerald Jack, Sports Information Director Larry White and photographer Kent Gidley.

Barker sat with Unitas.

Unitas, who played his college football at the University of Louisville, got to talk first. "We are here to honor a young man, Mr. Jay Barker, who has been most successful at the University of Alabama. He's had a fantastic career going 34-2-1. You are not that successful without great players around you and without you doing the job, and having good coaches to work with you."

To demonstrate the point, Unitas treated the crowd to a Barker highlight film that had been produced just for the occasion.

The Unitas Award is symbolized by a trophy in the shape of an arm, cocked and ready to throw a football. This Golden Arm Award goes each year to the nation's top senior collegiate quarterback

In 1994, Barker took the prize over Rob Johnson (Southern California), Chad May (Kansas State), Steve McNair (Alcorn

State), Kordell Stewart (Colorado) and Eric Zeier (Georgia). He was selected by a national committee of professional football general managers and player personnel directors, and members of the print and electronic media.

WHEN Barker got his chance at the microphone, he recognized those who had helped shape his life:

Jerome and Barbara Barker. "I feel like God has blessed me with the two greatest parents on the face of the earth. What you see tonight is because of them. They have invested so much of their lives in me."

Sister Andrea "who was the best athlete in the family" and his girl friend Amy "who has helped me get through my college career in the good and bad times."

Gene Stallings. "Y'all do not know what this man has meant to me, the things he has taught me off the field as well as on the field."

Quarterback coaches Moore and Smith for making him the quarterback that he became.

The Crimson Tide. "I dedicate this trophy to my team-mates," said Barker. "I love those guys with all my heart and without them, I wouldn't be here tonight."

THEN he added, "I just want to give all the praise, honor and glory to my Lord and Savior Jesus Christ. That's where all my strength comes from." He was interrupted by applause.

"My career hasn't been one of superstar status, I guess you might say. I've had a lot of criticisms. I came back this year from a knee injury and the season didn't start off as well as I wanted it to. I stuck to a verse that I shared on national television after the Georgia game. It is in I Peter 5:6-7 which says, 'If you humble yourself, therefore under God's mighty hand, he will lift you up in due time.' So I've stuck to that verse and God has lifted me up in due time. This is due time and I feel so privileged..."

Barker concludes his college career by thanking Alabama fans with a salute at game's end

CITRUS
BOWL

*H*ow could there have been a more fitting end? In the last minute on the last offensive play of his last game as the quarterback for the University of Alabama, Jay Barker threw a touchdown pass that won the game.

It was not without a little help from his friends. Actually, it came with a lot of help from his friends.

Running back Sherman Williams took the short Barker pass over the middle and outran the Ohio State team 50 yards to the end zone, and to a 24-17 victory over the Buckeyes.

After Alabama's previous 12 games Barker has trotted unemotionally to the dressing room, helmet off and, more often than not, with his index finger pointing skyward.

This time it was different.

BIRMINGHAM News writer Doug Segrest told the story. This time, Jay Barker let his emotions seize control, if only for a few moments.

After the rest of his teammates had headed into the Citrus Bowl locker room, Barker took a stand in an end zone, surrounded by Alabama fans screaming themselves hoarse in the wake of the Tide's come-from-behind...win. Standing marine-recruit straight, he locked both feet together and raised his right hand in a solemn salute to the crowd. Pivoting a few degrees to the left, he did it again and saluted another section of fans in the stands. One more pivot, one more salute to another legion of crimson-clad people.

Finally, he turned his salute hand into a fist and banged it against his chest, as if to reach his heart. Then he was off, under the tunnel beneath the grandstand.

"I was saying 'Thank you,' to the fans," Barker explained later. "They're out there all the time and I don't have a chance very often to show them how I feel about them. Alabama fans are the greatest fans of all time, and I wanted to let them know what they've meant to me."

Minutes earlier, Barker and his teammates had little time to bare their souls.

Having tied the game at 17-all with 4:29 left, Alabama had one final shot to win the game. After the defense had forced an Ohio State punt, Alabama took possession at its own 37 with 74 seconds remaining.

"We felt in the huddle we were going to win," Barker said. "The guys are very confident. We knew with 4 minutes left (when

Alabama tied the score) that we'd have another chance to win it."

On first down, Barker connected with Toderick Malone for a 13-yard pass. After an incompletion, he returned to the receiver who had opened the previous scoring drive by turning a short pass into a 41-yard gain.

The target: tailback Sherman Williams.

The idea was to clear the secondary out with three wide receivers going 15 yards deep. Williams would curl underneath, with the hope of drawing an Ohio State linebacker in man-to-man coverage.

Instead, Ohio State blitzed its linebackers, trying to deny Barker the time to locate a downfield receiver. Left to keep up with Williams was defensive end Mark Vrabel dropping off the line. While Vrabel had fared well in containing Williams at the line of scrimmage, he stood little chance in the open field.

"We'd had man-to-man coverage on the linebacker all day, and I'd been able to beat them," Williams said. "When I caught the ball and I saw it was man-to-man again, I knew we were in for a big play."

Needing 30 yards to get within reasonable distance of a Michael Proctor field goal to go ahead, Williams instead produced 50 and the go-ahead touchdown.

"This team has displayed the ability to come from behind," Tide coach Gene Stallings said. "That's a big advantage, when you know your team is not going to get flustered when they fall behind."

Fittingly, the go-ahead exchange came from seniors: Williams and co-captain Barker.

When Alabama dismantled Ohio State's final threat on the following drive, seniors again played a key role. Safety Willie Gaston knocked away a pass into the end zone with two seconds left and cornerback Tommy Johnson—like Barker, a co-captain—batted the game's final pass to the ground.

For the record, on his final day as Alabama's starting quarterback, Barker attempted 37 passes and completed 18 of them for 317 yards. He was not intercepted.

THE Ohio State win gave his senior class the school record for the most wins in a four-year period. They finished with 45 wins, five losses and one tie.

Before the Ohio State game they had been tied with the 1977-80 players who had a mark of 44-4-0.

"This senior class knew what we had to do," offensive tackle Joey Harville said. "We had to play with all our ability, and we pretty much have over the four years."

Several of the victories were comebacks. Five times in the 1994 season the Tide came from behind in the fourth period.

"We've been called the Cardiac Kids," Harville said. "When you come back and win a game, you work that much harder. We just thought we could win those games."

The key to Alabama's ability to come back this year, Harville says, was Barker's improvement.

"Jay improved so much. When you've got a quarterback like that, you know you can come back. We've seen Jay grow up over four years. He has gone from a no-name quarterback to a guy who makes plays.

"Hours after practice is over, he's still out working.

"He's a good Christian, and he believes God has given him his ability. He's just a leader. He doesn't stand for anything bad."

SO there he was at the end, standing on the floor of the Citrus Bowl in Orlando, Florida, saluting the Alabama faithful.

"I thought about waving," he said, "but I was afraid they wouldn't understand. So I decided to salute."

"It's a sad feeling, but I'm happy too," Barker said later. "And that my last collegiate pass was a touchdown—what a great way to end a career."

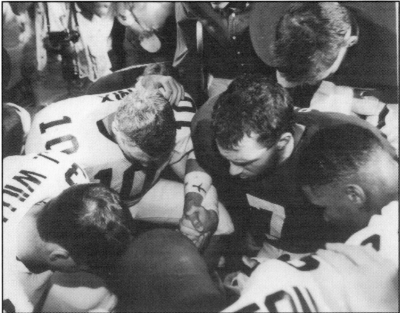

Post-game prayer is a tradition started at Alabama. Here Barker holds hands and prays with Patrick Nix and Frank Sanders after the 1994 Auburn game.

HONORS &
AWARDS

1994

- Johnny Unitas Golden Arm Award, top senior quarterback in the nation
- Street and Smith Exemplary Player of the Year for College Football
- Heisman Trophy finalist, fifth place
- Davey O'Brien Outstanding Quarterback finalist
- Maxwell Award finalist
- United Press International All-American, second team
- Associated Press All-American, third team
- *Nashville Banner* Southeastern Conference Player of the Year (head coaches)
- *The Birmingham News* Player of the Year
- All Southeastern Conference, first team (coaches, AP)
- Academic All-American
- Academic All-Southeastern Conference
- *Sports Illustrated* "National Player of the Week" versus Georgia
- ESPN's "Player of the Game" versus Georgia
- SEC "Offensive Player of the Week" versus Georgia
- SEC "Offensive Player of the Week" versus Mississippi State
- ESPN Scholar Athlete of Game versus Tennessee
- United States Sports Academy, Alabama Athlete of the Year
- Alabama team Co-Captain
- Butts Memorial Award by The Atlanta Touchdown Club as Outstanding Offensive Player in the Southeast
- Christian Athlete of the Year from Lay Witness International

1993

ABC's "Player of the Game" versus Tennessee

1992

SEC "Offensive Player of the Week" versus Mississippi

1994 HEISMAN TROPHY AWARD FINALISTS

1. Rashaan Salaam   Colorado
2. Ki-Jana Carter   Penn State
3. Steve McNair   Alcorn State
4. Kerry Collins   Penn State
5. Jay Barker   Alabama
6. Warren Sapp   Miami
7. Eric Zeier   Georgia
8. Lawrence Phillips   Nebraska
9. Napoleon Kaufman   Washington
10. Zach Wiegert   Nebraska

UNIVERSITY OF ALABAMA WINNINGEST QUARTERBACKS

Quarterback	Record	Pct.	Years
Jay Barker	35-2-1	.934	1991-94
Harry Gilmer*	30-9-2	.756	1944-47
Pat Trammell	26-2-4	.875	1959-61
Jeff Rutledge	24-4-0	.857	1976-78
"Dixie" Howell*	22-2-1	.900	1932-34
Mike Shula	22-8-1	.726	1984-86
Joe Namath	21-3-0	.875	1962-64
Terry Davis	21-3-0	.875	1971-72
Ken Stabler	19-2-0	.905	1966-67
Richard Todd	18-2-0	.900	1974-75
Steve Sloan	17-2-1	.875	1963-65

Gilmer and Howell played halfback in single-wing formations, but were their team's passer and ball handler.

JAY BARKER REGULAR SEASON
CAREER PASSING

Year	Games	Att.	Comp.	Pct.	Yards	Long	Int.	TD
1991	9	66	33	.500	554	75	3	1
1992	12	243	132	.543	1,614	46	9	7
1993	9	171	98	.573	1,525	59	7	4
1994	12	226	139	.615	1,996	74	5	14
Totals	42	706	402	.569	5,689	75	24	26

ALABAMA REGULAR SEASON
CAREER RECORDS

Most Yards Passing

5,689	Jay Barker	1991-94
4,899	Scott Hunter	1968-70
4,257	Walter Lewis	1980-83
4,069	Mike Shula	1983-86
3,842	Gary Hollingsworth	1989-90

Most Pass Attempts

706	Jay Barker
672	Scott Hunter
621	Gary Hollingsworth
578	Mike Shula
504	Walter Lewis

Most Pass Completions

402	Jay Barker
382	Scott Hunter
345	Gary Hollingsworth
313	Mike Shula
286	Walter Lewis

Most Consecutive Passes Completed

11	Jay Barker vs. Mississippi State, 1994
10	Gary Hollingsworth vs. Ole Miss, 1989
10	Gary Hollingsworth vs. LSU, 1989
10	Ken Stabler vs. Ole Miss (8) and Clemson (2), 1966
10	Jay Barker vs. Tulane (8) and Vanderbilt (2), 1993

Most Consecutive Passes Without An Interception

155	Jay Barker, 1994
100	Jeff Rutledge, 1977-78
100	David Smith, 1988
91	Steve Sloan, 1965

Barker Passing Statistics
With 30 or More Attempts In One Game

1992 vs. Ole Miss	25 of 39, 285 yards	1 TD	1 Int
1993 vs. Tennessee	22 of 40, 312 yards	0 TD	1 Int
1994 vs. Georgia	26 of 34, 396 yards*	2 TD	0 Int
1994 vs. Mississippi State	26 of 35, 325 yards	3 TD	1 Int
1995 vs. Ohio State	18 of 37, 317 yards	1 TD	0 Int
Totals	117 of 185, 1,635 yds.	7 TD	3 Int

(.632 percentage completions); 327 yards per game
*Second in Alabama history. Record by Scott Hunter, 484 vs. Auburn, 1969 (30 of 55).

ALABAMA RECORD WITH BARKER
AS STARTING QUARTERBACK

Year	Won	Lost	Tied
1991	4	0	0
1992	13	0	0
1993	6	1	1
1994	12	1	0
Totals	35	2	1

BARKER STARTING RECORD
VS. OPPONENTS

Team	Won	Lost	Tied
Arkansas	3	0	0
Auburn	3	1	0
Colorado	1	0	0
Florida	1	1	0
Georgia	1	0	0
Louisiana State	3	0	0
Louisiana Tech	2	0	0
Miami	1	0	0
Memphis State	1	0	0
Mississippi	3	0	0
Mississippi State	2	0	0
Ohio State	1	0	0
South Carolina	2	0	0
Southern Miss.	2	0	0
Tennessee	2	0	1
Tulane	3	0	0
UT-Chattanooga	1	0	0
Vanderbilt	3	0	0
Totals	35	2	1

Alabama records provided by University of Alabama Sports Information Department

ABOUT THE AUTHOR

WAYNE ATCHESON is Associate Director of the Tide Pride football donor program at the University of Alabama. He joined the athletic department staff in 1983 as Sports Information Director.

For the past 10 years, he has been advisor to the Alabama Fellowship of Christian Athletes Huddle.

He holds journalism degrees from Samford University and the University of Alabama. This is his third book. He has authored *Our Family Was A Team*, a story of faith and courage in his own family, and *Impact For Christ*, the 40-year history of the Fellowship of Christian Athletes.

His wife, Barbara, is a first grade teacher. Barbara and Wayne have two daughters, Elizabeth, a freshman at Samford University, and Amy, a sophomore at Tuscaloosa County High School.

Photo by Kent Gidley